play stronger, better, happier

A PRACTICAL GUIDE TO SPORT PSYCHOLOGY

ARNOLD LEUNES

This edition published in the UK
in 2018 by Icon Books Ltd,
Omnibus Business Centre,
39–41 North Road,
London N7 9DP
email: info@iconbooks.com
www.iconbooks.com

First published in the UK
in 2011 by Icon Books

Sold in the UK, Europe and Asia
by Faber & Faber Ltd,
Bloomsbury House,
74–77 Great Russell Street,
London WC1B 3DA
or their agents

Distributed in South Africa
by Jonathan Ball,
Office B4, The District,
41 Sir Lowry Road,
Woodstock 7925

Distributed in Australia and
New Zealand
by Allen & Unwin Pty Ltd,
PO Box 8500,
83 Alexander Street,
Crows Nest,
NSW 2065

Distributed in Canada
by Publishers Group Canada,
76 Stafford Street, Unit 300
Toronto,
Ontario M6J 2S1

Distributed in the USA
by Publishers Group West,
1700 Fourth Street,
Berkeley, CA 94710

ISBN: 978-178578-327-2

Typeset in Avenir by Marie Doherty

Printed and bound in the UK by Clays Ltd, St Ives plc

About the author

Dr Arnold LeUnes is Professor of Psychology at Texas A&M University in College Station, Texas. His main teaching areas are sport psychology and abnormal psychology, and his research focuses almost totally on sport-related issues. He has written a popular textbook on sport psychology as well as a reference work on psychological testing in sport psychology, published over 100 journal articles, and made well over 100 conference presentations. He is married to Judy, a community activist and animal and teacher advocate, and has six children, ten grandchildren, and two great-grandchildren.

Author's note

It's important to note that there is much frequently-used research employed in sport psychology. Where I know the source I have been sure to reference it, but my apologies here to the originators of any material if I have overlooked them.

Contents

1. The field of sport psychology: an overview

What is sport psychology?

Let's begin with a case study.

 Melanie is a talented 16-year-old long-distance swimmer whose short-term goal is to compete at the collegiate level, with an eye, long-term, on making the Olympic team. She has struggled of late with motivation and what appears to be burnout, and her coach is frustrated by her inability to rekindle Melanie's competitive fire. The two of them talk the situation over and agree that something has to give. This leads the coach to see if she can locate a sport psychologist to help Melanie get her competitive edge back.

The local phone books fail to turn up anything, but a call to a university athletic department points them in a potentially productive direction. The person they talk with says that there's a national organization devoted to sport psychology that, among other things, keeps a registry of sport psychology practitioners. Their website is a rich source of information about the field, including a list of potential sources of help in Melanie's area.

A phone call is made and the coach sets up an appointment for Melanie to talk with a sport psychologist specializing in staleness, burnout, and loss of competitive edge. Weekly counseling sessions, in which proven techniques and procedures are employed, eventually get Melanie back on track, and she resumes her training with the gusto of old.

The hypothetical case of Melanie serves as an introduction to what is known popularly as sport psychology, or more properly, **sport and exercise psychology**. This broader title emphasizes the twin challenges for professionals working in the field. Helping individual athletes and sport teams perform better is one of the many challenges for the sport side of the equation. On the other hand, using psychological principles to improve exercise adherence and enjoyment of physical activity illustrates a couple of the challenges facing the exercise domain.

Sport psychology is a specialty within the broader science of psychology. It emphasizes the relationship between **psychological** and **behavioral** principles that exert an impact on sport and exercise performance, and how these can be applied. When people contact a sport psychologist for whatever reason, it's expected that the professional will be able to perform a number of functions – and where they cannot, make an appropriate referral to someone who can.

Why do people need help from sport psychology?

- A common reason for seeking assistance from a sport psychologist is to improve sport performance. Athletes have sought the competitive edge since the ancient Olympic games in Greece, and a fair number think that sport psychology principles can assist them in accomplishing this aim.

- Another reason someone might seek sport psychological assistance is to manage interfering anxiety. Athletic events are sometimes heavy on stress and some athletes manage anxiety better than others. Most sport psychologists are well trained in the area of anxiety management.

- Yet another motive might be to help improve the sport experience for young people. As we'll see later, youth sport can be a real pressure-cooker for kids, and sport psychologists can contribute to a better sport experience for them.

- From time to time, athletes get injured, and sport psychologists are becoming increasingly involved in the rehabilitation process. There's an obvious physical component to a sports injury, but the recuperation process is often heavily psychological.

- Finally, the sport psychologist can put on his or her exercise hat and develop strategies for improving exercise adherence and enjoyment.

All of these topics are covered in the following chapters.

REMEMBER THIS!!! It's also highly likely that many of the things sport psychologists teach athletes will have application to other aspects of their lives. For example, learning to manage sport-related anxiety can have equal application to managing anxiety when taking important classroom examinations. The aim of this book, then, is to show how psychological principles are used, in practice, in sport and exercise settings, and how these same principles can often apply to everyday life events.

FAQ

Q. I'm considering pursuing a career in exercise psychology. Is there a resource I can consult to get a clearer picture of what the field is all about?

A. Bonnie Berger, David Pargman, and Robert Weinberg wrote a book on the topic entitled *Foundations of Exercise Psychology*, which was published by Fitness Information Technology in 2006.

Q. I want to keep up with daily developments in sport psychology. Is there a website that can do that for me?

A. Yes. Dr Michael Sachs at Temple University in Philadelphia moderates a sport psychology site. To subscribe to the website, contact Dr Sachs at: SPORTPSY@LISTSERV.TEMPLE.EDU

What do sport psychologists do?

Briefly, sport psychologists participate in three main activities: **teaching**, **research**, and **practice**. The first two, teaching and research, typically are conducted in conjunction with each other in the university setting. To get a feeling for these three activities in the work setting, let's look at typical days in the life of an academic and an applied practitioner.

A day in the life of an academic sport psychologist

Though things vary from day to day with teaching assignments and research duties, a typical day might be spent preparing for an hour or so for back-to-back classes, actually teaching those classes for two hours, then coming back to the office to meet with some research assistants. After lunch it's time for office hours, departmental meetings, maybe a consultation with an athlete, and perhaps some writing or preparation for an upcoming conference presentation. By then, it's time to head home for a meal and then back to school to make a presentation to a school group. By 9.00pm, the day is wrapped up with a couple of hours of family time.

A day in the life of the applied sport psychology practitioner

It's safe to say that one size doesn't fit all, so it's somewhat difficult to characterize a typical day in the life of a sport psychologist in private practice. Nonetheless, a day might begin by conducting individual and/or team performance enhancement sessions and, with the necessary credentials and training, providing clinical or counseling services to an athlete with personal problems. When not seeing clients, the applied person busies themself with documentation of sessions, writing or creative projects, and perhaps going out to a sports venue later in the day to watch some clients at their team practice. This might also result in consultation with coaches at the site.

Most (though not all) sport psychology courses and programs are found in Departments of Kinesiology or Movement Sciences, and yet a number of key positions, for example those found at the US Olympic Committee, require the practitioner to have the doctoral degree in the field of Clinical or Counseling Psychology and a license to practice in their state or province. Interested professionals in countries such as Australia, Canada, and Great Britain where the programs in sport psychology also have deep roots in kinesiology and movement science, have also been wrestling with this issue. To deal with licensing, divisions have been created within the psychological societies of those three countries to provide opportunities for professionals to express their opinions and enjoy the benefits of membership in such associations. Other countries with less well-developed sport psychology programs, such as those in Asia and Europe, are making progress in this regard.

The Appendices at the back of this book give fuller details of the history of sport psychology and of various key figures in the field.

FAQ

Q. I'm interested in finding a sport psychologist to work with my 14-year-old who aspires to be professional soccer player. Where do I go?

A. Consult the Yellow Pages in your local phone directory or call the athletic department at a nearby university to see if one is employed there. Or, alternatively, ask for the names of any coaches who have contracted on their own for sport psychological services. Try the Association for Applied Sport Psychology (AASP) website: http://appliedsportpsych.org

---

Why do we have sport psychology?
The field has developed for at least five major reasons.

One is **national identity** – nations pride themselves on their athletic accomplishments, and national esteem and validation of various political philosophies are often associated with athletic achievement.

Secondly, there is **money** in sport: it's a multi-billion-dollar enterprise with high stakes. Owners spend hundreds of millions or even billions today to purchase major sports teams; athletes are given massive salaries to ply their skills on the pitch, the diamond, the gymnasium, or the football field; golfers make millions trying to put the little white ball into the small, elusive hole.

A third reason for the emergence of sport psychology is the continuing growth of our **fascination with youth sports**. Millions of children all over the globe take part in sports, a movement with relatively recent roots and much attendant controversy.

A fourth reason for sport psychology is **spectatorship**. Fanatical sports fans are legendary and have been the subject of much speculation and some research of late, trying to figure out what makes sports so fascinating to them and why they behave the way they do at athletic events.

And finally, the **fitness movement** has added to the demand for sport psychology services, again to enhance both participation and enjoyment. It's this seeking of national identity, fame, money, youth sports enjoyment, spectatorship, and the pursuit of fitness that have elevated sport psychology to the status of major player in the worlds of sports and fitness.

Q. I'm interested in getting an advanced degree with a specialization in sport psychology. Where can I go to find information?

A. Fitness Information Technology in Morgantown, West Virginia publishes a *Directory of Graduate Programs in Applied Sport Psychology*, which is in its 9th edition as of 2008. Details of graduate programs in the US, Britain, Canada, and Australia and New Zealand are featured.

It's important to remember that sport and exercise psychology is a relatively new field that embraces both the domains of sports and fitness, and is made up of professionals from both kinesiology and psychology who, somehow, peacefully co-exist.

2. Reinforcement and punishment

There's no denying the fact that genetics exerts a powerful influence over human development throughout our lives. However, to gain a more thorough understanding of human behavior we need to be aware of the interplay between **reinforcement** (i.e. reward) and **punishment**. It makes absolutely no difference whether one is coaching young athletes, running a business, raising children, or commanding a military unit: the person with a thorough understanding of how to use reinforcement and punishment is going to be more effective in shaping desired behavior than someone who lacks this expertise.

What is reinforcement?

Reinforcement is defined as anything that increases the likelihood of a subsequent response. Key to understanding is the word 'anything'. A dog cookie may reinforce begging on the part of a hungry house pet; a pat on the back from a respected coach may increase the desire of a football player to excel; or, unfortunately, abuse can make a woman with low self-esteem come back for more abuse, despite well-understood undesirable consequences.

Types of reinforcement

Reinforcement may be primary or secondary, or positive or negative. **Primary reinforcement** is attached to some basic or biological need. Food when hungry and water when thirsty are prime examples. Also, the athlete who has had his or her breath knocked out knows the reinforcing properties of being able to breathe good old air! **Secondary reinforcement** works through association with primary reinforcement. A good example of secondary reinforcement is money: money takes on reinforcing properties not because it has any inherent value (you can't eat money), but rather due to its association with primary rewards such as food or sex. Medals, badges, trophies, public recognition, pats on the back, nods of the head, and an unanticipated smile from a beautiful woman or handsome man all qualify as powerful secondary reinforcement.

As for **positive reinforcement**, it increases desirable behavior through its presentation. A desirable behavior takes place and a reward is dispensed, thus increasing the likelihood that the behavior will occur again. The same result may be obtained through **negative reinforcement**, but the mechanism is more difficult to understand. Negative reinforcement increases the likelihood of recurrence of a particular behavior by preventing or avoiding a negative consequence. The end result is the same as positive reinforcement, in that the desired behavior is made more likely – for example in sports, because the athlete prevents or avoids something negative, such as the wrath of the coach.

It's common among laymen to equate negative reinforcement with punishment, but they are not one and the same. Negative reinforcement, again, implies avoiding or terminating a negative consequence, whereas punishment is the application of a negative consequence to prevent future undesirable behavior.

 You are the coach of a bunch of six-year-olds just learning the game of soccer. You know that being positive with young players is essential. But what positive procedures can you use? First of all, and most critical to success, is to create goals for each practice that set the players up for success. Know what you are trying to accomplish with each practice. Then, try a combination of positive approaches, such as instructions on what to do and how to do it, demonstrate proper technique, pass out compliments readily, and smile and pat people on the back when they do well. You might also set up a visible reward system (known as **public recordings**) with each player's name on a sheet of paper. You simply attach stars by their names when they perform skills correctly.

Enhancing the effectiveness of positive reinforcement

 The most important single thing to remember about reinforcement is simple in theory: **Positively reinforce those behaviors that you would like to see repeated**.

- **Make sure the reinforcement is in fact rewarding to the individual**. Athlete number one throws her trophies in the back of a closet and they never surface again. Athlete number two displays his awards in an elaborately designed trophy case. Obviously, one child values trophies, the other does not, thus the reward value differs.
- **Immediacy in applying the reinforcement is essential**. If a beginning soccer player makes a great pass leading to a goal by a team-mate, immediately tell him or her how great you thought the assist was.
- **Start out reinforcing desirable behavior every time it occurs**, then 'lean out' the schedule to make it more potent. Initially reward a beginning golfer for every shot that hits the green, but later, only those that land within twenty feet of the hole.
- **Use as many reinforcers as you can** to reward desirable behavior. Verbally reinforce desirable behavior for good plays, post team and individual results and highlights in public places, award performance-based T-shirts acknowledging extra effort and achievements of top performers, and highlight them in a student or local newspaper.

- **Make use of the Premack Principle** in which a preferred activity is used to reinforce one that is less preferred – for example, have periodic social gatherings (highly preferred activity) to reinforce the noon workout group (lower preference activity).
- **Encourage self-reinforcement and self-control**, as an internal guidance system is ultimately more effective than an external one. For example, discuss with your athletes the virtues of an internal dialogue, or self-talk, in which they reward themselves for positive accomplishments.

Contrasting coaching styles using positive and negative reinforcement

Positive reinforcement in coaching

John Wooden, the basketball coaching legend at the University of California at Los Angeles (UCLA), coached his teams to thirteen national collegiate championships largely through the use of positive incentives. Wooden was an All-American performer in his playing days, so he was able to **model** the desired sport skills for his players. Modeling is said to occur when the player simply observes the model doing something correctly, in this case Wooden himself. Wooden also placed strong emphasis on **instruction** about what to do and how to do it, sprinkling in liberal **verbal reinforcement** when players performed skills correctly.

However, Coach Wooden was not above using punishment when necessary. For example, an All-American player named Bill Walton returned to college sporting a beard of which he was justifiably proud. After letting the team practice for a while, Wooden called his star player over to discuss the new facial growth. Walton, a bit of a free spirit, reported that he was proud of the beard and declared it was his right as an individual to have one. Coach Wooden congratulated Walton on sticking to his beliefs and defending them when challenged, and concluded the conversation by telling Walton that the team would miss him. Walton promptly went into the dressing room and shaved off the prized beard. He was said to have phoned Coach Wooden weekly to talk and express his admiration until his beloved mentor died in 2010 at the age of 99.

Negative reinforcement in coaching
At the opposite extreme in terms of coaching style is the controversial British soccer manager, Sir Alex Ferguson, whose Manchester United teams have won numerous English Premier League championships under his authoritarian rule. 'Brick-minded', 'steely', 'short-tempered', 'ruthless', and 'controlling' are just a few of the terms used by the media to describe his 'my way or the highway' coaching philosophy. He's also well known for 'the hairdryer', a scalding, in-your-face blistering of players who offend him. Seemingly

untouchable players such as Wayne Rooney and David Beckham have felt his wrath, and his intimidation of referees has led to what is known as 'Fergie time', in which unusually generous injury time is added to the clock in matches where Manchester United is behind.

Both Wooden's and Ferguson's approaches produced multiple championships. Not surprisingly, Coach Wooden would disagree with terrorizing players to get them to perform well, and has been quoted as follows:

> *Motivating through fear may work in the short term*
> *to get people to do something, but over the long run*
> *I believe personal pride is a much greater motivator.*
> *It produces far better results that last for a much*
> *longer time.*

Continuous and intermittent schedules of reinforcement

The effectiveness of reinforcement, be it primary–secondary or positive–negative, depends on the schedule with which it's dispensed. There are two basic schedules: continuous and intermittent. A **continuous schedule** applies reinforcement 100% of the time – that is, every time the desirable behavior occurs, it's going to be reinforced. A good example in sports is coaching beginning athletes. With six- and seven-year-olds, it's likely that the coach will reinforce good dribbling in basketball or good passing in soccer every time they occur. However, as youth athletes continue playing, a continuous schedule loses its power to motivate. This means that coaches use less and less reinforcement, or what behavioral psychologists would call a 'leaner schedule'.

Once a desirable behavior has been acquired, it's best maintained through an **intermittent schedule**. Essentially, in an intermittent schedule, the athlete never quite knows when and where the reinforcement is going to be dispensed. Such a schedule may be based on time or it may emphasize work output, but for a behavior to continue in the long run it's important that reinforcement be dispensed unpredictably. Unfortunately, undesirable behaviors are usually maintained by intermittent schedules also, thus making them more difficult to modify or eradicate. Just ask any parent with a problem child or a coach with a troubled athlete.

Examples of intermittent schedules of reinforcement
As we saw above, an intermittent schedule of reinforcement is best for maintaining behavior. Accordingly, there are four intermittent schedules that have been used in sport psychology practice, and they are:

- **Fixed Ratio Schedule**. In this schedule, reinforcement is dispensed based on a fixed amount of work output. Producing a fixed number of running shoes on an assembly line or getting a helmet decal in football for performing well illustrates this schedule.

- **Variable Ratio Schedule**. Here, work output is still relevant but the schedule of reinforcement is variable and thus unpredictable. Anyone who has golfed, fished, or gambled on athletic events is quite familiar with this schedule.

- **Fixed Interval Schedule**. Here we are dealing with time as opposed to work output. An example is a set schedule for examinations and other assignments, say in a university course.

- **Variable Interval Schedule**. To illustrate this schedule, let's say that a track coach wants his quarter-milers at practice to run three back-to-back laps on the track at a 60-second clip. To vary the routine, he might have his runners do the first lap in 60 seconds, the second in 65, and the third in 55. The average is still 60 seconds but the pace for each lap is variable, thus adding variety and challenge to the practice.

The two variable schedules are most resistant to what is known as **extinction** (i.e. fading away) and are recommended over the two fixed schedules, which are susceptible to extinction if the reinforcement stops.

 Imagine you're a coach with a passable awareness of schedules of reinforcement that you picked up in a college psychology course. You know that variable schedules produce more long-lasting desirable effects than to fixed schedules. Thus, you shy away from rewarding your athletes after the performance of a certain number of desired skills. Rather, you reward your players sufficiently but on an intermittent schedule that is harder to predict. Your players will work harder and longer when they are uncertain about the schedule of reinforcement.

Q. Are there drawbacks to reinforcement? Can reinforcement get in the way of performance?

A. Yes, there are potential drawbacks. One is that reinforcement can potentially undermine the intrinsic joy of sports and fitness. Over-reliance on external incentives can cause drops in performance. Also, reinforcement can raise response rates beyond the optimal level, thus making a potentially enjoyable activity a chore or exercise in drudgery. Finally, some athletes may feel that they are being manipulated by the reinforcement regimen in place.

Punishment

Punishment, as we saw earlier, involves the application of a negative stimulus to modify or eradicate undesirable behavior. Knowing how and when to apply punishment is truly one of life's most important challenges in a most critical area: that of properly raising children. The same thing can be said for sports, though it's admittedly of lesser importance in the grand scheme of things. The good coach knows how to properly use reinforcement, positive or negative, but also has carefully delineated negative consequences for his or her athletes should it become necessary to use punishment.

It's a popularly held belief that misbehavior is eradicated through the use of punishment, but learning researchers long ago established the fact that punishment **represses** or **submerges** rather than eradicates. Thus, it's important when applying punishment to be aware that the recurrence of the undesirable behavior is always a possibility. So it's vital to use punishment to supply information when misbehavior is in remission, while at the same time providing desirable alternatives for the person being punished.

Providing a desirable alternative to punishment

Here's an example to which almost any parent can relate. It's perfectly acceptable to communicate to a child that he doesn't hit his little brother (for which he's being punished), but it's quite alright to take out his aggressions on the inflatable life-sized doll which takes a good wallop, falls backward, and kicks back up, ready to absorb another blow. In this case, the undesirable behavior has been identified and punished and a desirable behavioral alternative has been provided. The hope is that the strength of the reinforced desirable response will weaken the tendency to misbehave. To some this might look like eradication, but in reality it's repression. The layman can call it what he or she wants, given that the end result is the same: that is, the undesirable behavior is no longer being displayed.

Strengths and drawbacks of punishment

There are pluses and minuses associated with punishment, and the main strength lies in its capacity for repression of undesirable behavior. On the other hand, its weaknesses are numerous:

- One is that **punishment merely represses**, leaving the possibility of a later behavioral flare-up. Once again, misbehavior is never truly and fully eradicated; rather it's pushed below the level of observation, which is a good thing.

- A second negative associated with punishment is that it may **entrench** the very behavior it was designed to treat. Punishing toileting accidents in a toddler may entrench bedwetting rather than getting rid of it. Punishing the whiny brat for being whiny may reinforce being a whiny brat rather than treating the condition. Punishing a basketball player who also excels in distance running may actually increase the frequency of misbehavior at basketball practice because the player loves to run. Remember our earlier warning: 'anything' can be a reinforcer.

- Thirdly, punishment may be **dispensed too long after the occurrence** of the misbehavior. Punishing the happy, tail-wagging dog at 8.00am for urinating on the carpet at 3.00am merely tells the dog not to wag his tail and be happy early in the morning.

- A fourth shortcoming lies in its **emotional consequences**. Sometimes, the emotion involved can be so intense that the message about misbehavior gets lost in the shuffle of loud voices, threats, and spankings.

- A fifth is that a negative emotional state directed at the person dispensing the punishment may **generalize to all authority**. What elementary school teacher has not experienced a child who constantly breaks the rules, gets in fights, and causes general mayhem? More often than not, the source of the problem is easily traceable to an undesirable home situation, in which one or both parents are physically and/or psychologically abusive.

Most significantly, our world is beset with significant social problems that are related to lack of reinforcement for desirable behavior and indiscriminate use of punishment, physical and psychological neglect, and out-and-out cruelty. The streets of many cities are full of criminals who learned early in life to hate their parents or parent substitutes for cruel and unusual punishment. These same teenagers and adults take their hatreds out on society in ever-increasing numbers, with dire consequences for us all.

Punishment serves an important role in shaping individual and group behavior and truly has a place in the greater scheme of things. No business, school, home, or athletic team can successfully exist on positive incentives alone. Negative behavior will always occur and there will continue to be a need for punishing those who deviate from the rules.

 It's important to remember that if punishment is to be used effectively, it must meet three succinct and simple standards: punishment must be (1) **mild**; (2) **prompt**; and (3) **consistent**. Punishment that meets these three standards will always be more effective in shaping behavior than systems that deviate from these principles. Mildness keeps interfering emotion at a minimum, promptness closely ties the punishment to the misbehavior, and consistency keeps the intended message front and center at all times.

While genetics is always an important consideration when one considers human behavior, it's also greatly shaped by an interaction between environmental influences known as reinforcement and punishment.

Key figures

Ivan Pavlov (1849–1936). The Russian physiologist demonstrated through experimentation with dogs that people and other organisms learn through conditioning. His approach is known as **classical conditioning**.

John B. Watson (1878–1958). Watson was a professor at Johns Hopkins University in the early 1900s, and his experiments with a young male child, known in the psychology literature as Little Albert, demonstrated the **conditioned** nature of fear.

Burrhus F. Skinner (1904–90). Skinner was Professor of Psychology at Harvard University in the middle part of the 20th century, and his views on the interplay of reinforcement and punishment have been most influential in shaping our understanding of animal and human learning. His approach to learning is often referred to as **operant conditioning**, a view quite different from that of Ivan Pavlov. Pavlov viewed learning as a largely *passive* process, whereas Skinner thought of learning as an *active* process in which the subject operated on the environment or manipulated it, hence the use of the word 'operant'.

3. Arousal, anxiety, and their assessment

What is arousal?

Arousal is a state in which a person reacts to stress both physically and psychologically. The early research focused on a formulation known since 1908 as the **Yerkes-Dodson Law**, also known as the **Inverted-U Hypothesis**. Briefly, the Yerkes-Dodson Law states that the relationship between arousal and performance can best be visualized in terms of an inverted U-shaped curve. Putting performance on the vertical axis and arousal on the horizontal, one will find that performance is worse at low and high levels of arousal and best at some mid-point, thus yielding a performance–arousal curve shaped like an upside down or inverted U. Much research has been generated over the years by the Yerkes-Dodson Law.

Q. My football coach believes there are universal techniques that work in motivating our entire team. He tries to fire us up by giving emotional speeches, throwing tantrums, hurling objects across the dressing room, and so on. Some of my team-mates seem to really respond positively to these techniques. As for me, I find that quiet introspection prior to a game gets me ready to play. I don't think I'm alone in my view that not all athletes get psyched up the same. What does science have to say about this?

A. It's generally accepted that what inspires one person may actually decrease motivation and hinder performance in another. The inverted-U hypothesis suggests that one can experience too much or too little arousal, both of which will exert a negative impact on performance. There is an optimal level of arousal for every athlete conducive to peak performance, and the good coach is aware of these individual differences and takes them into account in motivating players.

Q. Okay. I'm a tuned-in kind of coach and I agree that individuals get motivated to perform in a variety of ways. From your experience as a sport psychologist, what are some of things I might do to make sure I'm individualizing my mental preparation strategies?

A. There are mental preparation strategies known as **psych-up strategies**, and they include:

1. Imagining that each breath taken in increases arousal.
2. Stretching to increase blood flow and body temperature.
3. Pre-competitive workout to achieve the inverted-U and to reduce anxiety.
4. Music.

5. Energizing imagery. Imagine you're a tiger or greyhound, or use heavyweight champion boxer Muhammad Ali's famous mantra: 'Float like a butterfly, sting like a bee.'
6. Energizing verbal cues, such as 'blast', 'power', or 'explode'.
7. Drawing energy from the environment. Use the national anthem or the sun or the flag as sources of energy.
8. Pep talks.
9. Bulletin boards with slogans and favorite sayings, or press clippings where opposing players say things about you or your team that get you fired up.

What is anxiety?

Mike is a 21-year-old competitor in basketball and has suddenly developed problems shooting free throws. He has earned some unwanted national notoriety with his inadequacies at the free throw line. He has hit only four of 37 free throws during the current season, thereby setting a national record. As a younger player, he was decent as a free throw shooter, making two-thirds of his attempts over a three-year period. Needless to say, Mike and his coach are perplexed but are at a loss as to what to do, so they agree to seek the services of a sport psychologist. It's decided that a good starting point would be to see if **anxiety** is the source of the difficulty. Accordingly, they start out using both physiological and psychological assessment devices.

Once assessments are made, the sport psychologist can plan possible treatments accordingly.

Anxiety is a sub-set of arousal, and is characterized by uncertainty, discomfort, apprehension, and a fear of the unknown. There are a couple of ways to view anxiety, and one of them is the **state–trait dichotomy**. State anxiety can be linked to identifiable life events such as a job or college interview, the kick-off before an important football game, or a long week of important and stressful final examinations at university. All of us are familiar with situations that create state anxiety. As for trait anxiety, it's persistent and enduring, or the 'real you', and is thus less affected by everyday life events. Trait anxious people are essentially that way all the time.

Another useful framework with which to view anxiety is the **cognitive–somatic dichotomy**. **Cognitive anxiety** is more mental, and is produced by the thought processes in our brain and characterized by worry and apprehension; whereas **somatic anxiety** is experienced more through bodily responses such as shortness of breath, muscular discomfort, or, as in the case of athletes, the jitters or 'butterflies' before an important game.

Q. I'm anxious all the time, and when things are going well I still find things to get upset and worry about. I know that I am, in the language of the psychologist, high in trait anxiety. What is the impact of trait anxiety on anxiety associated with everyday events, or state anxiety?

A. In general, high trait anxious people are always going to interpret everyday life events as more stressful than they really should. In the worst case scenario, a high trait anxious athlete would probably respond to pre-game jitters or butterflies with sleeplessness, digestive tract problems, vomiting, breathing difficulties, and the use of superstitious rituals to ward off the effects of anxiety.

How can anxiety be assessed?

There are essentially two major ways to measure arousal and anxiety. One method is through instrumentation that measures various **physiological** functions indicating arousal, such as heart rate or electrical activity within the brain. It's then possible to make some inferences about anxiety based on levels of measured arousal. A second mechanism is to employ paper-and-pencil **psychological** instruments that assess anxiety-based responses based on self-report.

Physiological assessment methods
There are six basic ways to measure arousal or anxiety physiologically, and they are:

1. **Electroencephalography**. This fancy word is abbreviated EEG and involves the assessment of electrical activity occurring within the brain. The brain produces alpha and beta waves, with alpha waves indicating relaxation and beta waves arousal.

THINK ABOUT IT

Imagine you're an athlete who has trouble relaxing before a competition. You think it's hurting your performance, so you consult a sport psychologist who is trained to use physiological assessments including EEG. Over a period of several sessions, the psychologist is successful in helping you control arousal-related beta waves in the brain, in favor of those related to relaxation, or alpha waves.

---

2. **Electrical properties of the skin**. Like the brain, the skin also produces electrical activity that can be measured through instrumentation. The idea here is that when a person is stressed, they will respond to a mild electrical current with increased sweat gland activity, thus increasing moisture on the skin. The ease with which the current moves along the skin can then be assessed as an index of stress.

3. **Heart rate**. Simply stated, increases in heart rate are related positively to arousal or anxiety.

4. **Blood pressure**. Increases in blood pressure are also positively related to arousal and anxiety.

5. **Electromyography** (EMG). Increases in muscular tension indicate arousal or anxiety, and can be measured through instrumentation.

6. **Biochemical agent assessment**. The presence of certain biochemical agents such as epinephrine, norepinephrine, and cortisol can be measured through analysis of blood or urine samples. Heightened levels of these agents in the blood or urine suggest increased arousal.

Strengths and weaknesses of physiological assessment

There are positives and negatives associated with all of the physiological procedures. **Strengths** include their independence from what the individual reports verbally about anxiety, which may or may not be accurate: physiological data do not lie. Secondly, these procedures may be used with almost any individual. Such things as intelligence, reading ability, good eyesight or hearing are not required. Finally, most of the physiological procedures can be used parallel to actual behavior, for example measuring the heart rate of a golfer while he is playing.

Disadvantages include the need for expensive equipment that may also be logistically difficult to use. Also, science has never come up with a satisfactory answer as to why some people channel stress through the respiratory system (i.e. asthma) whereas others do so through the circulatory (i.e. high blood pressure) or digestive systems (i.e. ulcers). Thus, what might work with one individual may be less productive for another, and vice versa.

Psychological assessment of anxiety

On the psychological side of the equation, we are essentially talking about paper-and-pencil assessment where self-reported presence or absence of anxiety is at the heart of the matter. The typical anxiety test is made up of words or statements to which individuals respond on a 'Yes/No' basis, or perhaps on a five-point rating scale ranging from 'Never' to 'Almost Never', 'Sometimes', 'Almost Always' or 'Always', or some such format.

REMEMBER THIS!!!

Typical psychological tests that assess anxiety

The sport psychologist interested in assessing anxiety has a nice group of tests from which to choose. One device is known as the **State–Trait Anxiety Inventory** (STAI), a brief measure, as the title implies, of both state and trait anxiety. Though not originally created with athletes in mind, the STAI has been used extensively due to the anxiety–performance relationship in sports. Another couple of related measures that are sport-specific spin-offs of the STAI are the **Competitive State Anxiety Inventory**

(CSAI), a measure of state anxiety and self-confidence, and the **Sport Competition Anxiety Test** (SCAT), a measure of sport-related trait anxiety. Yet another measure is the **Sport Anxiety Scale** (SAS), which assesses somatic and cognitive anxiety.

Pluses and minuses associated with psychological assessment

One of the strengths of psychological assessment is ease of administration and analysis. All the sport psychologist has to do is present an athlete with a questionnaire, an answer sheet, a pencil, and turn him or her loose. Once the results are obtained, the typical anxiety instrument can be scored in a matter of minutes. A second advantage is that large numbers of people can be tested at the same time. On the other hand, a huge disadvantage is that psychological assessment devices are subject to a number of honesty issues. Most paper-and-pencil psychological tests seldom include a foolproof method for determining whether or not subjects are being honest in responding. They may not really know how they feel, they may try to present an image that is not really them, or they may out and out lie in responding to the items.

Q. I'm a sport psychology graduate student with a serious interest in how anxiety affects performance. Who are the prominent people in anxiety and its assessment?

A. A good starting point would be **Dr Charles Spielberger** of the University of South Florida, who proposed the state–trait dichotomy and created the STAI to measure these qualities. Another important person would be **Dr Rainer Martens** of the University of Illinois, the owner and founder of Human Kinetics, the largest publishing house in the world devoted entirely to sports and fitness. Martens created both the CSAI and the SCAT to make Spielberger's formulations more applicable to sports. **Dr Ronald Smith** of the University of Washington has made numerous contributions to sport psychology, one of which was the SAS mentioned earlier.

In the next chapter we go on to explore the various treatments for anxiety in sports.

 Anxiety is a sub-set of arousal, both of which can be assessed with a variety of physiological techniques, as well as psychologically with paper-and-pencil self-report inventories.

---

4. Treatment of sport anxiety

Sources of anxiety in athletes

The inherent uncertainty associated with sports competition is one of its most redeeming features, yet it serves as a major source of anxiety for athletes. This charming but double-edged sword of inherent uncertainty has created stress among athletes and a correspondingly intense interest among sport psychologists concerning the relationship between anxiety and performance.

Q. Are there variables that predict sport-related anxiety?

A. Yes, there are. In the midst of this inherent uncertainty, age (youth versus adult), type of sport played (team versus individual), and level of athletic achievement (beginner versus advanced) are important anxiety–performance variables to consider. Youth athletes appear to be quite susceptible to what psychologists call **evaluative apprehension** – which is simply anxiety generated by concerns about what coaches, parents, and peers are going to think about their performance. Also, individual athletes such as gymnasts or golfers are always the focus of critical eyes, whereas team athletes' contributions are often more disguised or nebulous. Finally, as athletes become more advanced and sophisticated in the plying of their skills, they worry less about what others think.

However, even the most elite athlete is not immune to anxiety. Fear of debilitating or career-ending injury, concerns about coach–player communication, expectations related to team and individual success versus failure, money issues where professionals are involved, making the roster of a professional or Olympic team, and general threats to one's status can all cause even the most accomplished athlete to have anxiety that may interfere with performance and enjoyment.

Four models for treating sport anxiety

One of the most sensible formulations about anxiety reduction is that of the esteemed clinical/sport psychologist mentioned earlier, Dr Ronald Smith from the University of Washington. He says there are four models with which to view anxiety reduction, and they are the extinction, counter-conditioning, cognitive–mediational, and coping skills models, each of which is described below.

The Extinction Model. In this model, individual athletes are exposed to their fears in a safe environment but one in which they cannot escape or avoid. One such technique under the extinction model is known as **flooding**, in which the individual is inundated or flooded with his or her fears,

36

thus being forced to confront them head-on but in an environment conducive to anxiety reduction.

Imagine you're a basketball player who is a notoriously bad free throw shooter and known also to choke in key situations. Try the following flooding technique. Close your eyes and imagine failing miserably in a key game situation and feeling the rejection of team-mates, scorn by opponents, and disappointment among friends and parents. Add to this failure scenario by bringing into play as many sensory experiences as possible: sweaty palms, pounding heartbeat, the smell of the gymnasium, and the taste of sweat on your dry lips. Imagine your opponents smiling confidently, team-mates avoiding your gaze, parents and friends staring hopefully, and the crowd screaming 'You're going to choke.' Repeat this scenario over and over, flooding yourself with anxiety. At some point, you should start feeling immune to choking in pressure situations because the anxiety no longer evokes the response. Think how you could translate this to your own particular sport or activity.

The Counter-conditioning Model. This model counters anxiety through conditioning. The primary technique is known as **systematic desensitization**, which does exactly what it says: namely, systematically desensitizing the athlete to his or her anxieties. Most of the anxieties we face are dealt with in the natural environment, almost always in an unsystematic or even haphazard fashion. To put it another way, we manage to come to grips with most of life's anxieties through trial and error. In some instances, however, this approach doesn't work, and dealing with anxieties in a systematic fashion in the sport psychologist's office may be necessary.

THINK ABOUT IT

Counter-conditioning through systematic desensitization

We can probably all agree that anxiety and relaxation are incompatible. To put it another way, you can't be anxious if you're relaxed, and that's the basic premise behind **counter-conditioning**. Imagine that you're a troubled athlete consulting a sport psychologist who, as part of the treatment program, will set up a hierarchy of anxieties for you, each of which will be mastered through relaxation.

For example, try to visualize the national championship game two days hence. This scenario should evoke some anxiety but is low in the hierarchy. Once you report no anxiety associated with this event, you're ready to move to the next level, imagining waking up the morning of the big game and starting immediately to think about it. Again, once you feel no anxiety with these thoughts, the next step in the anxiety hierarchy is ready to be confronted. Imagine walking toward the arena on the day of the game. Step four in the hierarchy is to imagine sitting in the dressing room and listening to the coach talk about the importance of the upcoming game. Finally, you have to confront the ultimate anxiety situation, preparing to shoot a free throw with one second left in the championship game with your team trailing by one point. If you make both free throws, your team wins; if you make one, the game is tied and your team at least has a chance to win in overtime; if you miss both, the championship trophy and fan adoration are out the window.

By mastering these scenarios in the artificial environment of the sport psychologist's office, these newly gained anxiety management skills will generalize to real-life sport situations.

Incidentally, systematic desensitization is often employed to help people with a morbid fear of flying in an airplane. The technique lends itself well to resolving anxieties about flight in the structured, safe treatment environment.

The Cognitive–Mediational Model. To get a better feeling for where this model has come from, a little bit of history is in order. In the 1960s and 70s, **behaviorism** as advanced by Pavlov, Watson and Skinner, among others, dominated psychology. There was much emphasis on reinforcement, punishment, and classical and operant conditioning, with the idea that people were pretty much products of these forces. At the same time, how people thought or felt about things going on around them was in disrepute.

However, a reawakening of interest in thoughts and feelings (i.e. **cognitive psychology**) took place in the 1970s and 80s, and suddenly it became acceptable, perhaps even fashionable, to talk about mental interpretation of events. People were no longer conditioned automatons, but rather they were thinking, feeling organisms reacting based not totally on what happened to them but rather on their **interpretation** of life events. The Greek philosopher Epictetus (55–135 AD) said it nearly 2,000 years ago: 'Men are disturbed not by things, but by the way they think of things.' Out of this reawakening arose the cognitive–meditational model with its emphasis on mental interpretation as a critical determinant of response to life events.

The example I use to get the cognitive–mediational model across to my students is the death of a parent, something reasonably rare but not unheard of among 21-year-olds. Death of a parent is going to be traumatic for the vast majority of young people, who are often unfamiliar with losing someone of importance. It follows that how people react will be an individual thing subject to their own feelings and subjective interpretations.

I had a young man call me many years ago, announcing that his 39-year-old father, of whom he was immensely

40

fond, had perished in a plane crash. The funeral was set for three days hence on a Thursday, and the student indicated he would be in class the following day to take my major examination. I assured him I would be flexible in giving him a make-up exam considering the recent tragedy. Despite the fact that this 19-year-old and his 39-year-old father had been both father and son as well as best friends, this student was certain his father would want him in class, taking the exam as scheduled, and moving on productively with his life. Not only was he there but he made the highest grade on the exam.

So we have one interpretation of tragedy. Another is seen in a recent situation where a student found out that her mother had been diagnosed with inoperable cancer. Three weeks later, the mother was dead. The student in this instance asked me to allow her to make up any missed work, as the mother's death would require that she be away from school for ten days. It's not my place to pass judgment on the two cases, but they are clearly the result of two different interpretations of essentially the same event, namely the death of a beloved parent.

These student vignettes capture the essence of the cognitive–mediational perspective. Events do in fact evoke behavioral responses, but the nature and expression of them is going to undergo mental restructuring that is a highly individual thing.

The Coping Skills Model. The technique most associated with this model is called **Stress Inoculation Training** (SIT), which is the creation of a Canadian professor named **Dr Donald Meichenbaum**. The essence of his approach is teaching anxiety management through relaxation and liberal use of positive coping statements. The general idea is that learning to cope with lower-level anxieties 'inoculates' the athlete against higher-order ones. To put it another way, SIT exposes the athlete to stress in manageable but ever-increasing doses in hopes that mastering these anxieties will provide some immunity to later and perhaps more important stressors. SIT has been used effectively in exercise settings as well as the sports of basketball, distance running, gymnastics, and squash.

Stages of stress inoculation training
You can put SIT to work in resolving your own sport-related anxieties using a three-stage approach advocated by Meichenbaum:

1. A **conceptualization phase**, where you focus on becoming aware of how positive and negative thought, self-talk, and imagery influence your performance;
2. A **rehearsal phase**, in which you learn how to use positive self-statements and other coping skills; and
3. An **application phase**, where you practise these newly-found skills in graduated doses of anxiety-provoking scenarios.

THINK ABOUT IT

Imagine that your sport is soccer and you're blessed with an exceptionally powerful leg. Your coach wants you to score your share of goals and take penalty kicks during games or in cases of shootouts, but you have let him and the team down with erratic performances of late. The mere thought of taking a penalty kick causes you great, almost crippling anxiety. Your coach refers you to the team sport psychologist, who sets up a Stress Inoculation Training treatment program for you. In the **conceptualization phase**, you're taught to recognize situations that cause you anxiety and to understand its potentially interfering characteristics. Also, you learn how a positive perspective can be an asset to you. In the **rehearsal phase**, you're taught specific coping skills, and positive self-statements are continually developed and practised. For instance, you might say to yourself: 'Just relax. You can do this. You're well coached and have handled tougher situations than this before.' In the final or **application phase**, the psychologist exposes you to graduated doses of anxiety in imagined situations and gradually moves you from there to practising your acquired anxiety-management skills in actual soccer conditions. Continued use of newly-learned coping skills and positive self-statements are stressed in this stage.

A basic and important tenet of SIT is that these new coping skills that are helpful in improving performance by reducing sport-related anxiety will also generalize to other aspects of the athletes' life such as his or her studies. Thinking positively, avoiding negative thought processes, and having a 'can-do' attitude should apply to all aspects of an athlete's life, and SIT can play an important role in this process.

Key figures associated with stress-reduction models

Dr Joseph Wolpe (1915–97). A native South African who spent many years in the US, Wolpe is credited with popularizing the highly effective treatment procedure known as **systematic desensitization**.

Dr Donald Meichenbaum (b. 1940). Meichenbaum popularized **stress inoculation training**, which has been used effectively in many areas of clinical and counseling psychology, as well as in sports. Meichenbaum has been named one of the top ten clinical psychology figures of the modern era. He retired in 1998 from the University of Waterloo in Canada.

5. Optimism in sports and exercise

We are what we repeatedly do.
Excellence, then, is not an act but a habit.

Aristotle

If you dream it, you can do it.

Walt Disney

There's no way to put a price tag on the value of an optimistic perspective about life in general, and that same positive outlook is invaluable in sports. Athletes with an optimistic outlook on life and sport performance consistently outperform those with a less positive attitude.

 Characteristics of the optimistic athlete
According to sport psychologists Linda Bunker, Jean Williams and Nate Zinsser, the optimistic athlete is characterized as follows:

'Confident athletes think they can and they do. They never give up. They typically are characterized by positive self-talk, images, and dreams. They imagine themselves winning and being successful. They say positive things to themselves and never minimize their abilities. They focus on successfully mastering a task rather than worrying about performing poorly or the negative consequences of failure.

This predisposition to keep one's mind on the positive aspects of one's life and sport performance, even in the face of setbacks and disappointments, is a hallmark of the successful athlete.

'Critical to this control of cognitions is self-talk, and the key is to always accentuate the positive and not engage in self-defeating cognitions. At the same time, it is important to realistically assess successful and unsuccessful behaviors without engaging in counterproductive cognitive attacks on the self. It is okay to be critical of poor performance, say on a classroom test; "I did poorly because I failed to grasp some key concepts" is far preferable to judgmental thoughts like "I am obviously stupid or I would have done better on the test". Again, keep the emphasis on assessing behavior and stay away from self-condemnation; nothing constructive comes from such ideation.'

Positive psychology

The case for **positive psychology** has been presented most eloquently by Martin E.P. Seligman, a University of Pennsylvania psychologist. Positive psychology emphasizes optimism, happiness, transcendence, the nurturing of genius and talent, making ordinary life more fulfilling, engagement, enjoyment, and a life of affiliation and belonging. Seligman became a highly recognized name in psychology in the 1960s with his research on **learned helplessness**, a psychological condition created when people or animals feel they no longer have control over events in their lives.

When I think of learned helplessness and sports, I'm reminded of a coaching change involving football (the American version) that took place at a large, well known university some years ago. The newly hired coach followed one who had espoused a philosophy that you never tell a kid he did a good job, as 'he will turn on you in clutch situations'. The displaced coach believed that you get performance through negative incentives, threats, and when necessary physical abuse. The new coach, upon meeting the team, was heard to say: 'I've never seen a bigger collection of whipped dogs in my life.' What the new coach was really saying was that he had inherited a team in a state of learned helplessness.

Over the years, Martin Seligman abandoned his research on learned helplessness, refocusing his considerable energies on positive psychology. Seligman has spent the past several decades writing about learned optimism and conducting educational workshops teaching optimism to children.

Pessimists' and optimists' interpretation of everyday life events

Marilyn Elias, a writer for *USA Today*, put forth the following examples of how pessimistic and optimistic children interpret and respond to life events:

Bad events

Pessimist	*Optimist*
Teachers are unfair.	Mrs Carmine is unfair.
I'm a total clod at sports.	I stink at kickball.
I got grounded because I'm a bad kid.	I got grounded because I hit Michelle.

Good events

Pessimist	*Optimist*
I'm smart at math.	I'm smart.
Dad is spending time with me because he's in a good mood.	Dad loves to spend time with me.
I was voted safety patrol captain because the other kids wanted to do a nice thing for me.	I was voted safety patrol captain because the other kids like me.

Imagine for a second that you're a serious amateur tennis player (or you could substitute most sports) who has just been eliminated from the city championships in the third round. You have the feeling that your tendency to get down on yourself and using negative self-talk is holding you back in getting better at your game. So you decide to see a local sport psychologist who is familiar with the work of Martin Seligman on optimism. In talking with the psychologist, it comes out that you tend to explain your defeat in terms of **permanent**, **pervasive**, and **personal** (pessimistic) as opposed to **temporary**, **isolated**, and **external** (optimistic). You tell the psychologist that your defeat means that you will never have a chance to win the title again (permanent), it will probably cause you to have a bad week at the office (pervasive), and it all happened because you just aren't a mentally tough competitor (personal).

The psychologist gives you some tools to work with to change from a pessimistic to an optimistic **explanatory style**, known as Seligman's **ABCDE** process:

1. **Adversity** refers to actual negative events related to your tennis game, i.e. playing poorly and losing.
2. **Belief** refers to the self-talk that goes through your mind when you play poorly or lose. Are you talking in permanent, pervasive, and personal ways or are they temporary, isolated, and external?
3. **Consequences** has to do with the results of your self-talk. Are these initial, almost reflexive thoughts positive or negative?
4. **Disputation** is critical in changing your perspective. There are four ways that you can dispute your negative self-talk. One is with **evidence**. The idea that you are a

terrible player can be disputed since you have already won three previous city titles. Another is **alternatives**, whereby you explain poor performance not with doom and gloom but due to the fact that you were up all night with a very sick, feverish child. **Implications** refers to the fact that there might actually be some truth associated with your negative assessment. Maybe you just aren't the tennis player you used to be, and maybe going back to your second love of golf would be a good move. Finally, you could question the **usefulness** of your ruminations. Are these thoughts going to make you a better tennis player? If not, don't dwell on them.

5. After you have gone through various internal disputes with yourself, hopefully you will be **energized** to keep going in pursuit of the championship or, at the very minimum, feel better about losing it.

Cognitive control in sports

In sport psychology, applications of positive psychology and positive self-talk are manifested in three **cognitive control** procedures: thought stoppage, countering, and reframing.

Thought stoppage is designed to intervene in negative thought processes by using some mechanism that interferes with them. A simple thing to do when thinking negatively is to say 'Stop', which temporarily breaks the chain of negativity. Another simple mechanism to accomplish the same thing is to snap your fingers.

Thought stoppage: an example from golf

If you're a golfer and plagued with the normal negative thoughts when you play, here's something you might try to break the pattern of negativity. Before playing your next round, load 100 paperclips into the right pocket of your shorts or slacks. After a couple of holes, you encounter one where the green is surrounded by water, and your first thought is: 'Oh, boy! Here's a green surrounded by water. I'd better get out an old ball because I'll probably hit my shot in the drink.' At that point, stop, reach into your right pocket and move a paperclip to the one on the left side. The action of moving the paperclip temporarily interrupts the negative thought pattern. At the same time, replace the negative thought with some positive self-talk, such as: 'Hey, I've hit this green ten consecutive times from the fairway. Why should I worry about hitting the ball into the water?'

Linda Bunker, a sport psychologist from the University of Virginia, reported a real-life case study in which she asked a female collegiate golfer troubled by negative thoughts to fill up a pocket with paperclips before a practice round. The golfer was instructed to stop long enough to move a paperclip from one pocket to another each time she had a negative thought. Again, the idea was that the negative thought would be interrupted by the paperclip transfer. At the end of eighteen holes, the golfer had shot an 84 and had moved 87 paperclips from one pocket to the other. In other words, the golfer had just short of five negative thoughts per hole. It's hard to imagine Lorena Ochoa or Phil Mickelson engaging in such counterproductive thoughts, but then that's why those two competitors have been so successful.

Countering. In this procedure, the emphasis is heavily on countering negative thoughts and self-talk with positive ones. Instead of saying to yourself, 'I can't hit her pitches. She throws too hard', you would counter with, 'Yes, she throws hard, but I've worked hard on my hitting with the batting coach. I will hit!' Or, 'If I miss this penalty, all is lost' would be countered with, 'Just kick the ball like you always do. The worst thing that can happen is the team will lose the game. They don't banish soccer-players who miss penalties to Siberia!'

Reframing. The essence of reframing is to put a positive spin on negative thoughts, emotions, or physical sensations. For example, it's not unusual for athletes to experience 'butterflies' just before the start of a competition. Instead of seeing these butterflies as detracting or harmful, reframe them as unrelenting energy just waiting to be unleashed on the opponent. The baseball player who hasn't had a hit in 25 appearances at the plate is surely in a slump. Though there's no panacea for curing slumps, the player might shorten the duration by recasting the slump as merely a period or rest, or even rebirth from which you will rebound with a vengeance.

One of the best examples of reframing I have ever heard of comes from major league baseball and one of its premier players of two decades ago, Wade Boggs. It's a truism that major league hitters are in dire straits when the pitcher has them down no balls and two strikes, or the infamous 0-2 count. Major leaguers collectively hit around .180 on the 0-2 count but Boggs hit .309 under these trying conditions, which is quite good when you consider the fact that only a handful of players hit above .300 for the entire season. When asked what his secret was, Boggs replied to the effect that he had the advantage over the pitcher on the 0-2 count because he had just seen two of his best pitches. As most of us who have played baseball can attest, it's difficult to recast the 0-2 count as an advantage!

A parting thought on optimism

Viktor Frankl was a Viennese neurologist and psychiatrist who became a major spokesman for the existential movement in psychology in the 1950s and beyond. Frankl was incarcerated along with his family in various Nazi concentration or extermination camps during the majority of World War II. He spent most of his imprisonment in Theresienstadt but later was moved to Auschwitz and, finally, to Dachau near Munich, where he was liberated in April 1945. Only a sister survived with him, and she had moved to Australia prior to the Holocaust. Frankl witnessed incredible suffering during those years and he wrote extensively about it until the end of his life. His most famous book, *Man's Search for Meaning*, was a recapitulation of his experiences and reflections on those years. Of the experience, he wrote:

'We who lived in concentration camps can remember the men who walked through the huts comforting others, giving away their last piece of bread. They may have been few in number, but they offer sufficient proof that everything can be taken from a man but one thing: the last of the human freedoms – to choose one's attitude in any given set of circumstance, to choose one's own way. ...

'And there were always choices to make. Every day, every hour, offered the opportunity to make a decision, a decision which determined whether you would or would not submit to those powers which threatened to rob you of your very self, your inner freedom; which determined whether or not you would become the plaything of circumstance.'

Optimism, positive self-talk, and cognitive control through thought stoppage, countering, and reframing are important components of a positive outlook on life and sport performance.

Key figures

Albert Ellis (1913–97). Ellis is a leading figure in the history of clinical psychology and the architect of Rational Emotive Therapy (RET).

Viktor Frankl (1905–97). Frankl's epic struggle for survival during the Holocaust greatly shaped his view of man's existence and led him to write his most famous work, *Man's Search for Meaning*. He practised psychiatry in the US after World War II.

Martin E.P. Seligman (b. 1942). Seligman is best known for his work on learned helplessness and learned optimism. He is currently the Director of the Positive Psychology Center at the University of Pennsylvania. He is the author of twenty books and 200 journal articles.

6. Mental toughness in sports

My greatest point is my persistence. I never give up in a match. However down I am, I fight until the last ball. My list of matches shows that I have turned a great many so-called irretrievable defeats into victories.
Bjorn Borg, professional tennis player

Mental toughness separates mountain people from valley people.
Frank Dick, UK athletics coach

I've missed over 9,000 shots in my career. I've lost almost 300 games. I've been trusted to take the game-winning shot ... and missed. I've failed over and over again in my life. And that is why I succeed.
Michael Jordan,
American professional basketball icon

Mental toughness is a state a mind you could call character in action.
Vince Lombardi,
National Football coaching legend

It's all about the top two inches.
Idiom, New Zealand
All Blacks rugby union team

What makes up mental toughness?

Mental toughness is widely accepted as a core component of the make-up of elite performers. Famous athletes who have been deemed mentally tough by their peers, coaches, or the media are numerous, and Michael Jordan of the US in professional basketball, Michael Schumacher of Germany in Formula One racing, Alastair Cook and Kevin Pietersen of England in cricket, Tiger Woods of the US in golf, and Shane Warne of Australia in cricket often surface when the topic of competitive grit or toughness comes up.

Dr Coleman Griffith of the University of Illinois is widely regarded as the 'Father of Sport Psychology'. During his tenure as Director of the Sport Psychology Laboratory at Illinois, he published two books, *Psychology of Coaching* (1926) and *Psychology and Athletics* (1928). Though he never made specific use of the words 'mental toughness', he did compose a list of traits he considered to be characteristic of the superior athlete. Thus, we can probably give Griffith at least part of the credit for initiating inquiry into the elusive nature of mental toughness. Forty years after Griffith's books were published, Dr Thomas Tutko, a Professor at San Jose State University in California, used the term 'mental toughness' in reference to the characteristics of elite athletes.

Personality characteristics of elite athletes

Coleman Griffith (1926, 1928)	**Tutko and Associates** (1969)
Alertness	Aggressiveness
Buoyance	Coachability
Conscientiousness	Conscientiousness
Courage	Determination
Emotional adjustment	Drive
Exuberance	Emotional control
Intelligence	Guilt proneness
Loyalty	Leadership
Optimism	*Mental toughness
Respect for authority	Self-confidence
Ruggedness	Trust

A more contemporary framework for understanding mental toughness comes from Drs Graham Jones, Sheldon Hanton, and Declan Connaughton in England. Their studies of world-class athletes, coaches, and sport psychologists from all over the world in the early 2000s led them to conclude that mental toughness is made up of four major components, with a variety of sub-components:

1. **Attitude/Mindset** – unshakeable self-belief, an inner arrogance, and desire and hunger.
2. **Training** – the mentally tough performer has patience, discipline, self-control, loves the parts of training that hurt, and thrives on opportunities to beat others in practice.

3. **Competition** – loving pressure, coping with adversity, being totally committed, having a killer instinct, possessing total focus, and controlling the environment.
4. **Post-competition** – celebrating and handling success and using failure to drive oneself forward in the future are hallmarks of mentally tough performers.

Jones and his colleagues asked ten world-class athletes to rank twelve statements they thought best described or defined the mentally tough performer, and they were:

1. Having an unshakeable belief in your ability to achieve your goals.
2. Bouncing back from performance setbacks as a result of increased determination to succeed.
3. Having an unshakeable self-belief that you possess unique qualities and abilities that make you better than your opponents.
4. Having an insatiable desire and internalized motives to succeed.
5. Remaining fully focused on the task at hand in the face of competition-specific distractions.
6. Regaining psychological control following unexpected, uncontrollable events.
7. Pushing back the boundaries of physical and emotional pain, while maintaining technique and effort under distress.

8. Accepting that competition anxiety is inevitable and knowing that you can cope with it.
9. Thriving on the pressure of competition.
10. Not being adversely affected by others' good and bad performances.
11. Remaining fully focused in the face of personal life distractions.
12. Switching a sport focus on and off as required.

Mental toughness: the integration of major league baseball

A strong argument can be made that the mentally toughest athlete of all time was Jackie Robinson, the black baseball player who was selected to integrate American major league baseball in 1947. One has to understand the depth and breadth of the racial hatreds, tensions, and upheaval taking place in the US at the time to get a true feeling for Robinson's toughness. He was shunned by many team-mates, not allowed to stay with his team in hotels or eat with them in restaurants, was harassed during the games by fans, and received innumerable death threats in person or through the mail.

Branch Rickey was General Manager of New York's Brooklyn Dodgers and he opted to integrate baseball with the carefully chosen Robinson. Robinson was no shrinking violet when it came to standing up for himself, but Rickey saw in him those traits that would be necessary to withstand the torrent of abuse in store for him. The exchange between the two mentally tough individuals here is legendary. Rickey said to Robinson: 'We can't fight our way through this, Robinson. We've got no army. There's virtually nobody on our side. No owners, no umpires, very few newspapermen. And I'm afraid the fans will be hostile. We'll be in a tough position. We can win only if we can convince the world that I'm doing this because you are a great ballplayer and a fine gentleman.' Rickey went on to detail the problems he foresaw, and told Robinson he literally had no choice but to respond to the abuse by turning the other cheek and enduring the indignities without reprisal. To this admonition, Robinson said: 'Mr Rickey, are you looking for a Negro who is afraid to fight back?' Branch Rickey's terse but telling reply was: 'Robinson, I'm looking for a ballplayer with guts enough not to fight back.'

The road to success was a long and rocky one, but Jackie Robinson went on to win over his team-mates, most of the fans, and many in the press. He paved the way for integration of sports in the US, and it could not have been done by someone with less mental toughness.

Assessment of mental toughness

Two sport psychologists, Dr Robert Harmison of James Madison University in the USA and Dr Michael Sheard of York St John University in England, are among those who have been trying to define and measure mental toughness.

Harmison has developed a paper-and-pencil instrument, the **Mental Toughness Questionnaire** (MTQ), which is 50 items long and attempts to measure five aspects of mental toughness: Tough Beliefs, Tough Attitudes, Tough Skills, Tough Values, and Tough Emotions. Michael Sheard's scale, the **Sports Mental Toughness Questionnaire** (SMTQ), is much shorter, only fourteen items in length, and assesses Confidence, Constancy, and Control:

Confidence
1. I interpret potential threats as positive opportunities.
2. I have an unshakeable confidence in my ability.
3. I have qualities that set me apart from other competitors.
4. I have what it takes to perform well while under pressure.
5. Under pressure, I am able to make decisions with confidence and commitment.
6. I can regain my composure if I have momentarily lost it.

Constancy
7. I am committed to completing the tasks I have to do.
8. I take responsibility for setting myself challenging targets.
9. I give up in difficult situations.
10. I get distracted easily and lose my concentration.

Control
11. I worry about performing poorly.
12. I am overcome by self-doubt.
13. I get anxious by events I did not expect or cannot control.

14. I get angry and frustrated when things do not go my way.

Former major league baseball player and manager Carl Kuehl, and two colleagues, have a different view of mental toughness than our more research-oriented sport psychologists. However, as you will see, there are some points of overlap, too. To Kuehl, mental toughness is a skill to be learned and developed, as opposed to being a talent or gift from nature.

REMEMBER THIS!!! You can learn to apply Kuehl's ideas on mental toughness to your own sporting endeavors. For him, mental toughness means choosing to take control of one's abilities and striving to succeed. Mental toughness …

- Is the difference between being talented and merely being successful
- Is the mindset to overcome obstacles
- Is an inner strength that creates resolve and dedication
- Is the understanding that achievement rarely comes without enormous hardships along the way
- Means keeping your head about you when others around you are losing theirs
- Finally, it is a conscious decision to be successful.

CASE STUDY

Carl Kuehl was asked by the Minnesota Twins baseball franchise to do some trouble-shooting with four of their key young players who were new to the league, kicking up their heels, staying out late and partying hard, and generally soaking up the perks associated with the money and glory of being a major leaguer. They were eventually called on the carpet by management and asked to party less and work harder at baseball. Accordingly, with Kuehl's help, the four culprits arrived at a mental toughness list to govern their future efforts. Their list included the following:

1. I will be ready to play and be my best every day.
2. Nothing will distract me from quality practices and pre-game routines.
3. I will play hard every day.
4. I will intimidate if necessary, and I will not be intimidated by anyone.
5. No matter what happens, I will keep my poise and act appropriately.
6. I will look like a professional and I will act like one.
7. I will be a good team-mate.

To make a long story short and provide a happy ending, the players turned their behavior around and all four enjoyed long and productive careers.

Fostering mental toughness

There's not much literature available on how to develop mental toughness. No doubt, there are child-rearing procedures that must have some impact, but the literature on precisely what these procedures might be is also sparse. In his 2010 book titled *Mental Toughness: The Mindset Behind Sporting Achievement*, Michael Sheard suggests that self-discipline and rational thinking must always win out over emotional reactions if one is to be mentally tough.

Components of mental toughness

Enormous self-discipline and willpower are essential components of mental toughness, and these two qualities are promoted by:

- Developing competence
- Always doing the 'right thing'
- Staying steady
- Resisting pressure
- Doing quality work
- Developing a positive sense of worth and self-confidence
- Conquering emotions through rational thinking
- Developing persistence
- Having career goals
- Learning to say 'no'
- Never ever allowing anyone to mentally cripple you.

It's incumbent on parents, teachers, coaches, and others to assist in the development of these important psychological skills. As well, the individual athlete must take responsibility for working on his or her own mental toughness.

> *Keep away from people who try to belittle your ambitions. Small people always do that, but the really great make you feel that you, too, can become great.*
> Mark Twain

 Defining mental toughness is difficult, but there is general agreement that determination, unshakeable self-belief, insatiable desire, resolute focus, competitive arrogance, and coping with adversity are core components.

7. Attribution theory and locus of control

THINK ABOUT IT

Think of yourself as a novice tennis player. In the process of learning the game, you are constantly confronted with trying to explain to yourself and others why you have enjoyed such early success. One explanatory mechanism is talent: 'I do well because I'm good at what I do, even for a beginner.' Alternatively, you could fall back on intense effort as an explanation: 'I work harder than my opponents who are also learning the game.' A third way for you to view success is to see the task as simply not too difficult: 'For me, tennis is simply easy.' Finally, you could invoke luck as being on your side: 'I do well because I seem to always get the lucky bounce during important matches.' All of these explanations are called **attributions** in the language of the sport psychologist.

Attribution theory

As humans, we are always analysing our own behavior, trying to account for why things happen as they do. These explanations, or **attributions** in the language of the psychologist, help us achieve a certain degree of psychological closure, maintain integrity and self-esteem, and create order in our environment. Some attributions are causal and others dispositional. **Causal attributions** have to do with the reasons something happened, or the causes. For instance, you may explain your success in doubles play by asserting that you and your partner are simply better than the opponents at the game of tennis. As for **dispositional attributions**, we are talking of some trait or characteristic that can be used to explain success. Francisco might explain his prowess in tennis as the result of his being a mentally tough competitor, which is a dispositional inference.

One of the most influential researchers in the area of attribution theory was **Dr Bernard Weiner**, whose main work took place in the mid-1970s. Weiner developed a simple formula to account for the outcomes of human behavior. In its simplest form, Weiner said that task outcome (O) in achievement-related activity (for example, sports) is a function of ability (A), effort (E), task difficulty (T), or luck (L). You as a budding tennis star would likely view success or failure in a given tennis match based on some combination of perceived ability, the amount of effort exerted, the difficulty of the task at hand, and the strength and direction of luck or chance factors.

Four attributional components
Let's take a look at each of these four components to get a better feel for attributions for success and failure.

- **Ability**. Ability is something an athlete possesses – that is, it's internal. Ability can no doubt be enhanced by proper devotion to physical fitness, skills acquisition, and proper use of mental skills, but there's a substantial innate aspect to it. At the same time, ability is generally stable, thus changing little regardless of task outcome.

- **Effort**. Effort, too, is internal but it's unstable. How hard an athlete works can vary all over the place, and is a huge part of explaining wins or losses. One of the major challenges of coaching is to keep the individual and team effort constantly at the optimal level. At the elite level, the mentality of the typical coach is: 'I may not be able to control some things, but no coach will ever outwork me.'

- **Task difficulty**. I think we could all agree that running a sprint is easier than running the same distance over hurdles. Hitting a baseball is probably quite a bit more difficult than throwing one. Hitting penalty kicks in soccer is no doubt more difficult that passing the ball to a team-mate in the open field. Some things are simply easier than others. In general, the difficulty of a particular task is unchanging but external to the athlete.

- **Luck**. Luck or chance factors figure into sport event outcomes all the time. Wind, rain, snow, a chance call by an official, or a strange bounce of the ball are chance events that are hard to control and often used to explain wins and losses in sports. Luck is both external and unstable: you just never know when it will appear.

 Another way to look at attributions is along a dimension of **controllability**. Ability, for instance, is pretty much beyond the control of the athlete: you are what you are. Task difficulty is also largely uncontrollable. The difficulty in hitting a good backhand shot in tennis doesn't fluctuate – it, too, is what it is. Luck, on the other hand, fluctuates all over the place, and is thus uncontrollable. There's not much one can do about inclement weather, a referee's bad call, or a strange bounce of the ball. One thing that is controllable is effort: the individual player has control over how hard he competes.

 Coaches love slogans, and one of their favorites applies here: 'The harder I work, the luckier I get.' This is their way of convincing their athletes that effort is of paramount importance and luck is not as uncontrollable as one might think.

Another interesting aspect of attribution is what is known as the **self-serving attributional bias**, whereby success is attributed internally (i.e. ability, effort) and failure externally (i.e. task difficulty, luck). The purpose of this bias is to protect the ego in the face of failure.

Locus of control

Locus of control is a psychological term that refers to how people view control over events in their lives. As opposed to attributions, where they are explaining *why* things happen, the individual here is concerned with their individual control over events. Locus of control theory and research began at Harvard University in the 1960s with the work of **Dr Julian Rotter**, who suggested that people possess either an **internal** locus of control or an **external** one. An internal person would see themselves as determining their fate when dealing with life events. On the other hand, the external person would see other people or luck, or both, as influential in determining reinforcement in their lives. As part of his work, Rotter developed a paper-and-pencil test to assess internality or externality.

In the early 1970s, **Dr Hannah Levenson**, then a Professor at Texas A&M University, added some nuances of her own to Rotter's work as part of her doctoral dissertation. Levenson saw internality pretty much the same as Rotter but she believed the external dimension had two sub-dimensions, **powerful others** and **chance**. She believed that a person who was external but high on powerful others was a different person than an external with a high luck or chance orientation.

Q. I'm studying sport psychology and I need to come up with a proposed study in which the measurement of locus of control is essential. Any hints as to the best instruments available to me?

A. There are several assessment tools, and two of the best are those of Rotter and Levenson. Both have enjoyed a good reception from other psychologists with an interest in the area.

I-E Scale. Rotter's scale is 29 items long. Each item is made up of a pair of statements from which the respondent has to choose one. The totality of their responses determines internality or externality.

IPC Scale. Levenson's scale is composed of 24 items arranged along a seven-point scale indicating amount of agreement or disagreement. When the items are scored, the individual will have three scores: one for internality, one for powerful others, and one for chance.

It's important to note that everyone has elements of internality and externality in their interpretation of life events – no one is purely internal or purely external. You can view yourself as being pretty much in control of your life and yet be aware that we all have powerful others to consider, namely employers, coaches, priests or ministers, or the police. It's a rare athlete who doesn't understand the power that a coach has over his or her life, particularly as they move up from beginner to elite performer. Also, it would be disingenuous to rule out the role of luck in sports and life. Being in the right place at the right time when opportunity knocks is an important determinant of success.

A sport study of locus of control

Thirty years ago, my esteemed colleague Dr Jack Nation and I set out to see if we could develop a prediction system linking psychological variables to performance in the American brand of football. Our idea was to test all players for fifteen minutes each Wednesday and compare the psychological profiles we obtained with previous performance data compiled by the coaches for each player. Using a complex statistical formula, we planned on presenting each coach with a printout the next day that would predict the caliber of play on Saturday, or game day, of every player on the team. We used a popular test of mood state (see Chapter 11) and Levenson's locus of control scale.

Five years after the data was originally collected, we subjected it to a number of analyses and came up with a couple of interesting findings. One was that our black football players possessed significantly higher Chance scores than did white players. We viewed this as evidence that the black players generally came from the inner-city poverty areas of Houston and Dallas, where life truly is more a matter of chance than in the white suburbs. Gang activity, drive-by shootings, and endless drug deals on the streets can make you think that life is truly a game of luck or chance.

We also determined which of the entering freshmen at the time we originally collected the data had stayed with the team for their allowed five years, and which had departed. The first group was called 'Stayers' and the second 'Leavers', and our analyses showed that by combining the two scales, we could predict ahead of time who would leave the program and who would stay with 86.7% accuracy. In other words, we could predict with almost 90% accuracy who was going to stay and who was going to leave before these players ever played a down of football at the university.

Imagine that you're a college football coach. Your sport psychology research team has implemented a sophisticated prediction program that can predict with 90% accuracy who is likely to stay with your program for four years and who is not. You're told that your star recruit, a 'can't miss' prospect at the key position of quarterback, has the profile of a predicted leaver. What do you do at this point? Do you let events run their natural course with a 90% chance you will lose this star player soon? Do you call in an applied sport psychologist to work with the player? Do you yourself intervene and make the star player a special project of your own? These are just some of the possibilities open to you, and none is guaranteed to be successful. But at least the system allows for such identification, at which point you can put in place whatever measures you think best.

 Ability, effort, task difficulty, and luck attributions allow us to make sense of events affecting our lives. At the same time, how we view reinforcement or control of events is also a significant determinant of personality and behavior.

---

8. Leadership, group cohesion, and audience effects

Leadership, group cohesion, and audience effects are three important areas within **social psychology**. Let's take a brief look at how these areas of inquiry apply to sport psychology.

Leadership

It's almost impossible to view a televised team sport activity without hearing the announcers make some mention of the leadership qualities of one or more of the players. Player leadership, while often mentioned in the media, hasn't been studied thoroughly by sport scientists and remains a mostly unexplored area. On the other hand, quite a bit of research has been conducted looking at the coach as leader.

Studying coaching leadership in sports has been anchored for three-plus decades by Packianathan Chelladurai (aka 'Chella' to his peers and students) of the Ohio State University. His approach is known as the **Multidimensional Model of Sport Leadership**, and he proposes that leader performance and follower satisfaction depend on the way in which actual, required, and preferred leader behaviors mesh together.

- **Actual behaviors** are just that: the behaviors that the leader engages in irrespective of norms or preferences.
- **Preferred leader behavior** refers to those actions the followers would like to see in a leader.
- **Required behaviors** are those expected of a leader, such as organizational demands.

 Chelladurai's **Leadership Scale for Sports** (LSS) is composed of 40 items measuring five dimensions of leadership. If you're a coach or leader in sports, see if your work matches up in these five broad areas:

1. **Training and instruction behavior**. Here, demanding physical training standards are implemented, the skills and tactics of the sport are taught, and team relationships and interactions are structured and coordinated.
2. **Democratic behavior**. This means allowing players to have some say about group goals, practice methods, and game tactics and strategies.
3. **Autocratic behavior**. Stress here is placed on independent decision-making and personal authority. There's always going to be some need for these traits in order for an organization to function efficiently.
4. **Social support behavior**. Here, the emphasis is on the coach showing concern for his or her athletes and fostering good social relationships among team members.

5. **Rewarding behavior**. Recognizing and rewarding desirable behaviors are key aspects of this leadership dimension.

The LSS has been used widely and its validity, reliability, and utility within sports leadership have been demonstrated.

A major player in leadership evaluation and training in sports is **Jeff Janssen** of Janssen Peak Performance (www.jeffjanssen.com). He has studied leadership for years and has developed a scale for its assessment. His scale has 24 items on which leaders evaluate themselves on a five-point scale. The first half of the test measures four sub-components: Commitment, Confidence, Composure, and Character, which he calls **Leader by Example**. The second half of the test is called **Vocal Team Leader**, with sub-components of Encourager–Confidence Builder, Encourager–Refocuser, Encourager–Team Builder, and Enforcer. Janssen says that scores between 24 and 89 indicate the person is not a leader at all. Scores of 90–105 suggest the person is a solid vocal leader, and 106 to 120 are scores of spectacular vocal leaders.

THINK ABOUT IT

Let's say that a player gives himself a 115 but his coaches see him as an 87 and his teammates view him as an 85 on the Janssen scale. Clearly, there's a gap between the way the player views himself and how he's seen by others. It's

Janssen's experience that nine out of every ten athletes who aspire to be leaders are '**awareness challenged**'. Janssen suggests that it's incumbent on the coaches to then teach the player the skills and insights necessary to assume a position of leadership. As well, Janssen says that regular qualitative and quantitative feedback is essential. In the case of quantitative feedback, he recommends periodic use of his scale.

Janssen conducts annual workshops all over the US in cases where coaches and athletes want to go above and beyond in developing team leaders.

Leadership models within psychology

Much literature has been devoted to leadership in the broad field of psychology, particularly those aspects dealing with business, industry, or the military. Several models for viewing leadership have evolved over the years, and some of the more well-known are:

- **Trait Theory**, also known as the 'Great Man' theory. This model assumes that leadership is a trait that will make one a leader in most or all situations. The only trait to continually receive research support is intelligence, and it's a weak relationship at best.

- **Behavior Theory**. This approach emphasizes what the leader actually does rather than what he or she is.

- **Contingency Model**. This model places much emphasis both on characteristics of the leader and also on those of the situation. Task-oriented or **autocratic leaders** and relationship-oriented or **democratic leaders** are emphasized in this model.

- **Path–Goal Theory** presupposes that the main function of the leader is to stay out of the way and remove obstacles, thus providing a 'well-lighted path' for subordinates.

- **Life Cycle Theory**. Much emphasis in this model is placed on subordinate maturity and the ability of the leader to harness subordinate energies.

- **Functional Model**. Leaders are seen here as task-oriented (**instrumental**), or interpersonal, emotional, and social (**expressive**). It's not unusual in coaching to find task-oriented head coaches pairing themselves with an expressive assistant who tends to the social, emotional, and interpersonal needs of team members.

Group cohesion

All that year, the animals worked like slaves. But they were happy in their work: they grudged no effort or sacrifice, well aware that everything they did was for the benefit of themselves and those of their kind who would come after them.
George Orwell, *Animal Farm* (1946)

Harmony isn't important. All that matters is winning and getting paid.

Charles Barkley,
former professional basketball player

One year we had six guys in jail. Not together, because that would have meant teamwork.

Jon Spoelstra, President of
the NBA New Jersey Nets, 1993–95

Coaches, players, and sports commentators often invoke group cohesion or team harmony to explain success in sports. The Pittsburgh Pirates of major league baseball are often cited as an example of the positive outcomes of team cohesion. Their theme song, 'We are Family' by Sister Sledge, became the team mantra, playing continuously throughout their successful run to the World Series title in 1979. On the other hand, there are examples in which groups have excelled despite an apparent lack of team harmony. The Oakland A's of major league baseball in the 1970s fought continually on and off the field while winning three consecutive World Series titles in 1972, 1973, and 1974.

The word cohesion is derived from the Latin *cohaesus* which means to cleave or stick together. Albert Carron, a sport psychologist from Canada specializing in studying group cohesion, defines cohesion as follows: 'Dynamic process that is reflected in the group tendency to stick together while pursuing its goals and objectives.' He suggests that there are three major conceptual issues related to group cohesion:

1. Does cohesion develop in progressive, linear fashion once the group is established (i.e. the **linear model**)?
2. Does cohesion oscillate like a pendulum throughout the group's life cycle (i.e. the **pendular model**)?
3. In a group's life cycle, is there an increase in cohesion, a leveling off, and then a decrease as the group dissolves (i.e. the **life cycle model**)?

The linear model in practice

The linear model was formulated in 1965 by Dr Bruce Tuckman, who talks of **forming**, **storming**, **norming**, and **performing**. Let's assume you're the captain of a newly-formed cricket team. Your role as captain is to be aware of the processes that will take place as the team develops, and you're also responsible for putting into practice the four-stage process suggested by Tuckman's linear model of group cohesion. This is how the model works in practice:

- During the **forming** stage, the players get to know each other and learn the task demands ahead of them.

- The **storming** phase is characterized by polarization, rebellion, and conflict while players are sorting out roles and personalities.
- In the **norming** stage, the group comes back together as a cohesive unit, thus allowing them to move on to ...
- The **performing** stage where team goals are pursued in a cohesive fashion.

The pendular model is associated with S. Budge's work in 1981. Budge suggested that groups oscillate from cohesion to differentiation to conflict to resolution (i.e. cohesion) to conflict to resolution, and so on. Budge predicted that a team would spend the entire season in a pendular cycle of conflict to cohesion to conflict to cohesion.

In 1964 Theodore Mills proposed a life cycle model with five stages: (1) encounter; (2) testing of boundaries and creation of roles; (3) creation of a normative system; (4) production stage; and (5) separation and dissolution as the life cycle of the team plays itself out.

Factors affecting group cohesion

Group cohesion is affected by variables such as group size, the task itself, team tenure, and satisfaction. In general, it's easier to facilitate team cohesion in smaller groups. Of particular interest to sport psychologists is a phenomenon known as **social loafing**, or the decrease in individual effort resulting from the presence of co-workers or team-mates.

USEFUL TIP

We're all familiar with the group project in which there are eight members, one or two of whom end up doing all the work, though the others are quick to claim credit despite minimal effort and input. Imagine you have been put in charge of an eight-person team and want to get equal involvement of all participants in order to avoid the problem of social loafing. To ensure that all are pulling their weight, you should devise ways to make individual effort identifiable, keep group identification high, keep lines of communication open, be aware that motivation may wax and wane from time to time, provide occasional breaks in activity, and impress on each group member the admonition offered by sport psychologist Dr Charles Hardy: 'Somxonx will notice if you don't do your bxst.'

Task demands do make a difference in cohesion, simply because different sports have different degrees of team involvement. Some sports, such as soccer, American football or cricket, are considered to be **interactive** and demand a lot of team interaction and cooperation. Other sports such as golf and archery may have a team component but they are still largely individual, or **coactive**.

The length of time a team stays together can exert a profound impact on cohesion. In this regard, sport psychologists talk of **team half-life**, or the amount of time it takes the roster of a team to turn over due to attrition by

50%. Related to this is winning, and successful teams in general stay together longer, a probable indicator of team cohesion.

USEFUL TIP Imagine that you have two very good friends on your advanced youth soccer team, and are pretty much fed up with their pronounced tendency to pass to each other to the detriment of other players. You're convinced their friendship is costing your team goals in critical situations. To break up this monopoly, you should stress to them the importance of keeping all team-mates involved, separate their playing positions to minimize their selfish tendencies, and assign them to separate rooms when the team travels so that they develop other strong and productive relationships with team-mates.

Finally, **satisfaction** exerts some influence on cohesion, but the relationship is a tricky, chicken-before-the-egg one at best. Briefly stated, the argument goes: Does cohesion lead to satisfaction or does satisfaction lead to cohesion? This direction of causality has triggered much discussion and research, and its many nuances are beyond the scope of this book.

Audience effects
Audience effects operate as a two-way street. In one direction are the effects an audience has on performance, and in

the other the effects of competition on the audience, aka the fans. With regard to the first question, it seems safe to say that audience influences on a beginning athlete are largely negative (what is known in psychology as **evaluative apprehension**), may be either slightly positive or slightly negative on an intermediate performer, and are positive with the highly skilled athlete.

Real-life sports events are characterized by an interactive effect: the fans affect the behavior of the players and vice versa. Sport psychologists are interested in this give and take relationship between fans and athletes. Take, for example, the **home advantage**. It's a generally accepted axiom that the home team, all other things being equal, has an advantage associated with playing in their home venue. They are performing in front of mostly friendly fans, know their venue well from practice and games, aren't fatigued from travel, slept in their own beds the night before, and so on. These things add up to a subtle home advantage. In general, research supports this home relationship in a variety of sports including baseball, basketball, cricket, soccer, softball, wrestling, and the summer and winter Olympic games.

Interestingly however, there is research suggesting that there may actually be a **home disadvantage** in critical games. Analyses have been made of the final games of the baseball World Series and the National Basketball Association (NBA) championships. Using fielding errors as an indicator of stress, the home team in the final game of the World Series makes more errors than the visitors. In basketball, the home team shoots free throws less accurately than the opponents. Both situations can determine the outcome of critical games, and the results suggest a home field disadvantage. This is thought to be related to pressure on the players exerted by adoring fans.

REMEMBER THIS!!! Another interesting study focuses on **Basking in Reflected Glory** (BIRGing). BIRGing is related to the glory by association that fans receive from identifying with a winner. Research indicates that, for example, university students in the US are prone to wear significantly more school-related paraphernalia – caps, socks, sweaters, T-shirts and shoes with university logos on them – to class on Mondays after winning football games. Conversely, they wear less gear identifying them with their school after losses. We all like to be associated with a winner, and the research on BIRGing has supported this relationship with actual data.

There are many other aspects of the fan–athlete relationship that could be explored but time and space again limit the conversation. Suffice it to say that the fan–athlete interaction makes for some interesting discussions. As we shall see in the chapter on violence and aggression, this relationship is not always a healthy one.

IF YOU REMEMBER ONE THING Leadership, group cohesion, and audience effects are three important components of the social psychology of sport.

9. Team building and goal setting

> *He set the tone: it's about sacrifice. It's not about the player's name on the back of the uniform. It's about the name on the front: Texas. We've all said that we'd do this as a group, not as individuals.*
> University of Texas basketball player
> Royal Ivey, speaking of Coach Rick Barnes

Team building and goal setting are two major sport psychology topics and both are essential aspects of team effectiveness and player satisfaction. The two concepts are at once separate and yet interdependent, and there's a rich professional literature associated with both areas. Also, it's difficult to talk about team building without considering team cohesion, discussed in the previous chapter. Team cohesion and team building have much in common.

Team building

Team building is defined in general as a process whereby team unity and togetherness are promoted, thus enabling the team to run more smoothly and effectively. It has been suggested by a number of sport psychology authorities that the process of building an effective, cohesive team takes place either **directly** or **indirectly**.

REMEMBER THIS!!!

In the **direct intervention approach**, the sport psychologist actually works closely with the players in an attempt to educate them directly about the numerous subtle nuances associated with the creation of an effective, cohesive team. Any number of teaching approaches may be used here, and the emphasis is on establishing a climate of trust and open communication.

In the **indirect intervention approach**, the sport psychologist instructs coaches and managers about the most effective techniques and tools they can use with their athletes to help them create and maintain a cohesive team environment. It's then up to the coaches or managers to implement these various team building strategies.

Team building interventions for sport teams

In his very popular textbook entitled *Sport Psychology: Concepts and Applications*, sport psychologist Dr Richard Cox of the University of Missouri suggests thirteen strategies and interventions for building a psychosocially cohesive unit:

1. **Acquaint each player with the responsibilities of other players.** One tactic that could be used to accomplish this goal is to allow players to play positions other than their usual ones during practice. Example: a soccer player who is occasionally critical of a team-mate's

success in penalty shootouts would be given opportunities during practice to assume this critical and tension-filled role.

2. **As a coach or teacher, take the time to learn something personal about each athlete on the team.** Knowing something about a player's life goals, his or her relationship with parents, a nickname, or a favorite hobby can often open up the dialogue between coach and athlete, thus adding to the overall feeling of belonging to the unit.

3. **Develop pride within sub-units of large teams.** American football lends itself nicely to this idea because there are two distinct units within every team, one that plays exclusively offense and one that plays only defense. Familiarizing each of these units with the nuances and responsibilities of the others could go a long way in forging team unity. In sports such as basketball or volleyball, the number of players is smaller, the sub-units less distinct, and the application of this principle less clear.

4. **Develop a feeling of 'ownership' among the players.** Allowing players to have some say-so about team rules and procedures gives them an opportunity to buy into the team. At the same time, players will choose to see the team as their own rather than the exclusive property of the coaches or team management.

5. **Set team goals and take pride in accomplishments.** More will be said about goal setting shortly, but the successful team is one that sets attainable goals, works diligently toward them, and sets up a reward structure to recognize team and individual accomplishments.

6. **Make sure that each player on the team learns his role and believes it's important.** One of the great challenges of successful coaching is keeping each player happy with his role on the team, be it superstar or last man off the bench. Most basketball teams, in critically important games, only play eight, nine or ten of the twelve to fifteen players on the roster. Getting those other seven to ten players who seldom play to see that they contribute greatly by making practices tough and game-like can give them a sense of importance and a feeling that they make a contribution to team goals. Phil Jackson, the immensely successful coach of the NBA Los Angeles Lakers, puts it this way: 'I knew that the only way to win consistently was to give everybody – from the stars to the number 12 player on the bench – a vital role on the team.'

7. **Do not demand or even expect complete tranquility.** Given the nature of people, it's reasonable to expect that there will be ripples of disharmony from time to time on any given team. There are as many personalities as there are positions on the field, and getting them all on the same page can seem as difficult at times

as trying to herd cats. Just knowing that there will be occasional displays of disharmony is a first step toward achieving harmony. Also, it's important to remember the old military adage that when the troops aren't griping, you as the commander may well have a serious morale problem on your hands; the same goes for sports teams.

8. **Since cliques characteristically work in opposition to the task goals of a team, avoid their formation where possible.** Constant losing, unmet player needs, lack of playing time, and coaches who scapegoat certain players can contribute to disharmony and the formation of team cliques. Coaches should be alert to the formation of cliques and exercise care in dealing with them when they do form.

9. **Develop team drills that encourage member cooperation.** For example, soccer drills to develop individual excellence are obviously necessary, but setting up exercises that encourage team cooperation and unity are important.

Lack of cooperation: soccer

Carlos and Ian are best friends and play on the same club and high school soccer teams. They pass to each other during games to the exclusion of other team-mates and ultimately to the detriment of team success. Wide open players who might have a great chance to score are ignored as the two friends play favorites with each other. The coach decides at the next practice that he's going to separate the two by both distance on the field and playing position during drills, so that they may get the feel of passing the ball to other team-mates. His goal is, of course, to get them out of their comfort zone with each other, thus making the team more effective and increasing team morale among members who are turned off by what they see as the selfishness of Carlos and Ian.

---

10. **Highlight areas of team success, even when the team loses a match.** Citing some outstanding defensive plays by goalkeepers and defenders in a soccer game in which the team lost can turn a negative into a positive as the team moves forward to its next match.

11. **Work to develop collective self-efficacy (team efficacy) in the team.** By self-efficacy, we are referring to a generalized belief about success. Efficacious individuals and teams are convinced that they will win and otherwise be successful. One way to create this efficacy, or 'can-do' attitude, is to bring teams along slowly at first, making sure they are not overmatched by superior opponents. Winning feeds on itself, and creating a schedule that is not overwhelming but at the same time

offers sufficient challenge is the ideal, particularly with young or inexperienced teams.

12. **Develop a mastery motivational climate for the team.** The coach here attempts to create an environment where the emphasis is on mastery of skills and opponents rather than divisive team competition. Learning, mastery, and cooperation rather than excessive rivalry among team members is critical here.

13. **Educate the team as to the destructive effects of jealousy and how to avoid it.** Incorporating the previous twelve strategies will go a long way toward downplaying individual and counterproductive emotions that evoke jealousies that are detrimental to team performance and cohesion.

Sasho Cirovski: an important lesson in team building

For the 2001 season, University of Maryland soccer coach Sasho Cirovski appointed his best two players as co-captains. The team floundered along with a so-so season, and Coach Cirovski decided that things had to change. Desperate to resolve the leadership vacuum and salvage the season, he brought in his brother Vancho, a human resource specialist for a Canadian corporation, to assess the situation. Brother Vancho determined that the team leadership rested not in the best players but in a seldom used sophomore player, who the rest of the team all looked up to for his athletic and personal characteristics. His name was Scotty Buete and he was installed at mid-season as a third captain.

Cirovski then instigated a number of team building procedures including moving all players back on campus to live, making room-mate assignments that he thought promoted cohesion, recruiting future players based more on how they fit in than on sheer talent, and not bringing any new players to the team for a year, so as to not interfere with the newly-found team cohesion. Team cohesion and morale improved instantly, and Maryland went on to reach the final four at the national tournament that year and for each of the next three years, culminating in a national championship in 2005.

What a great example of team building!

Team building in fitness and exercise settings

Professor Albert Carron of the University of Waterloo in Canada is perhaps the leading authority in sport psychology concerning group cohesion, its assessment, and its application in both sports and exercise settings. In conjunction with several Canadian colleagues, Dr Carron has created some sound strategies for team building in the fitness setting. Their formulation is made up of five factors as follows:

1. **Distinctiveness**. The exercise group can be made distinct or unique by having a group name, creating a group T-shirt, equipping exercisers with neon headbands or shoelaces, and making up slogans and posters for the class.

2. **Individual positions**. The exercise leader should create distinct locations within the fitness setting that correspond to levels of fitness of the group members, label them accordingly, and encourage every participant to stay in the designated fitness group until they are clearly ready to move up.

3. **Group norms**. The emphasis here is on having each group member get to know as many of their exercise peers as they can. Introductions should be made initially, members encouraged to adopt each other as 'fitness friends', group goals delineated, and a group work ethic established and modeled by the leader.

4. **Individual sacrifices**. Members are asked to sacrifice for the sake of the group on random days through such things as more mat work or engaging in more aerobic exercises. Also, old members are asked to help the new people to become 'fitness friends'.

5. **Interaction and communication**. In this instance, group solidarity is enhanced through partnering up to demonstrate activities or to provide group reinforcement for working out.

It seems clear that team building in the sport and fitness domains is an important activity, one that can enhance sport performance and physical fitness, and the enjoyment of both.

Goal setting

If people knew how hard I worked to get my mastery, it wouldn't seem so wonderful after all.
Michelangelo Buonarroti,
sculptor, painter, architect, and poet

It's no secret that coaches want players to set goals for themselves, and it's easy to assume that the process is a simple one: the player sets goals and the player achieves them, thus relieving the coach of being an active participant in the process. On the other hand, the coach who is on top of the intricacies of goal setting knows it's not simple at all. There are many things to consider in making goals realistic and achievable.

There have been well over 100 published studies of goal setting, and a number of conclusions have been made that are applicable to sports. Among them are:

- Specific, difficult goals lead to better performance than vague, easy goals;
- Short-term goals can be used effectively to achieve long-term goals;

- Goals affect performance by promoting effort, persistence, and direction of attention, and by motivating strategy development;
- In order for goal setting to work, feedback concerning progress is essential;
- Goals must be accepted if they are to affect performance in a positive direction.

SMART goals

H.W. Smith, a writer, has proposed a framework for looking at goal setting that emphasizes the creation of SMART goals:

S Goals must be **specific** or spell out clearly what is to be accomplished;

M Goals must be **measurable** or quantifiable in some fashion;

A Goals must be **action**-oriented and relevant to the task at hand;

R Goals must be **realistic**, sensible, and capable of being carried out;

T Goals must be **timely** and capable of being accomplished within a reasonable time-frame.

Three types of goals

Experts on goal setting talk of three types of goals: **outcome** goals, **performance** goals, and **process** goals.

Outcome goals are those most closely associated with team or individual achievement, or to put it another way, winning. There are certainly other outcome goals, but winning is very often paramount among coaches and players, though as we shall see in a later chapter, outcome goals appear to be of lesser importance to youth athletes.

Performance goals are typically separate from other performers or the total team. Scoring a hat trick (such as making three goals in a soccer game or taking three wickets with consecutive deliveries in cricket) might be a performance goal, though few players probably ever achieve such a standard. Shooting a round of 80 in golf, scoring 20 points in a basketball game, or completing 70% of one's passes in football are examples of other performance goals. One of the nice things about performance goals is that they often lead to the achievement of outcome goals. Another plus is that greater personal satisfaction may result from the achievement of performance goals even when outcome goals are less successfully met. As a caveat here, anyone who has played or watched sports closely knows that when a player places a higher premium on his or her own performance goals to the detriment of team outcome goals, morale problems and loss of team cohesion are just around the corner.

Finally, **process goals** place a premium on proper performance of skills associated with a particular sport. Thus, keeping the left arm straight when hitting a golf ball, watching a baseball pitch all the way to the bat, or getting a perfect spiral on a pass in American football are all examples of process goals. Obviously, proper skill execution can lead to improved performance with regard to performance and outcome goals.

 Applications of goal setting

Goal area	Goal
Psychological skills training	A long jumper imagines successful completion of a personal best; he engages in appropriate self-rewarding statements.
Individual sport skills	A youth golfer sets a goal for the summer of reducing the average number of putts to complete nine holes from 22 to 18.
Team sport skills	A Little League team sets a goal for the season to reduce errors from four per game to two per game.
Physical fitness	A 65-year-old sedentary man with high blood pressure sets a goal of reducing his resting heart rate from 80 to 60 in one month using yoga and relaxation training.

Goal area	Goal
Physical health	A recent heart attack victim sets a goal of losing three pounds per month for a year; she rewards herself every three months with some new clothes reflecting the incremental weight loss.
Personal satisfaction	A middle-aged but competitive softball pitcher sets a goal of making at least three positive self-statements per game suggesting that the game is fun, not World War III.

Trouble areas in goal setting

There are a number of problem areas in goal setting that merit the attention of the coach, player, and sport psychologist. One concerns the creation of poorly written goal statements. In accomplishing this most important first step, it's prudent to remember the use of SMART goals.

A second pitfall in goal setting is the failure to devise effective goal attainment strategies. If a striker in soccer is to improve his game over the off-season (if there is such a thing any more), it's not enough to say, 'I'm going to get better at putting the ball in the net.' It would be more effective to say: 'I'm going to' …

1. Shoot on goal alone for twenty minutes a day three times a week.
2. Practise dribbling and one-on-one moves twenty minutes a day three times a week.

3. Work on improving my first step quickness by engaging in an exercise and stretching regimen three times a week.
4. Practice shooting on goal against a live goalkeeper 30 minutes once a week.
5. Watch English Premier or Bundesliga soccer in the soccer channel whenever possible.
6. Use visualization to perfect successful shots five minutes for each of the three days leading up to an important match.

Simply put, if goal attainment strategies are to be successful, the plan must be followed. For example, even the most sophisticated and well-developed weight loss plan is doomed to failure if the person involved isn't deeply committed to its success. Being unable to walk away from the candy counter without a chocolate bar in your hand can spell disaster for the best planned fitness regimen.

Properly monitoring progress is a necessary next step in successful goal setting, and it may take the form of some of the techniques discussed in Chapter 15 on exercise and fitness, namely self-monitoring and stimulus-cueing.

Finally, setting goals that are too difficult, emphasizing outcome goals over performance and process goals, and having too diverse an array of goals can all hamper goal attainment.

REMEMBER THIS!!! Two important subject matter areas in sport psychology are team building and goal setting. Effective teams make liberal use of sport psychologists and/or techniques they have developed. As well, successful teams engage in planful goal setting. The same principles that apply to sports teams have equal application in the fitness and exercise setting.

10. Aggression and violence in sports

I speared him, I pole-axed him, and I cut him close to the eye. Things like that happen in the heat of the game.
Unnamed ice hockey player

Serious sport has nothing to do with fair play. It is bound up in hatred, jealousy, boastfulness, disregard of all rules and sadistic pleasure in witnessing violence. In other words, it is war minus the shooting.
George Orwell

A society that presumes a norm of violence and celebrates aggression, whether in the subway, on the football field, or in the conduct of its business, cannot help making celebrities of the people who would destroy it.
Lewis Lapham (b. 1935), editor and writer

Our sports arenas are truly forums for aggressive behavior and violence, from the bleacher bums at American sports events to the soccer hooligans of Britain. Hardly a day passes when there isn't a media report of a fight at a sporting event or an American collegiate athlete beating up a team-mate, fellow student, or more likely, a girlfriend.

What constitutes aggression?

Aggression is derived from the Latin 'to walk toward'. It's defined in four steps:

1. The delivery of a negative stimulus;
2. with intent to do harm;
3. to an unwilling victim;
4. with the expectancy of success.

Q. I have twisted my knee pretty badly playing soccer and just got back from a visit to my orthopedist. He grabbed my knee and twisted it in a variety of directions, some of which were quite painful. Why was he being so aggressive with me?

A. In the technical language of the psychologist, the doctor was not being aggressive because he meant no harm. Rather, he had to inflict some pain on you in order to make the correct diagnosis.

Aggression can also be understood in terms of looking at what reward the aggressor expects to gain from his or her efforts. Three kinds of behaviors are relevant to this discussion:

1. **Assertive behavior**. In sport assertion, the athlete intends no harm, uses legitimate force, and engages in an unusual expenditure of energy or force.

2. **Instrumental aggression**. In order to qualify as aggression, the intent to do harm must be present. In this type of aggression, the intent is to win and there is no anger.
3. **Hostile aggression**. Once again, the intent is to do harm, but the goal is also to harm (winning is coincidental), and there is anger.

 I'm reminded here of an incident I witnessed at a college football game several years ago. A wide receiver for Team A ran downfield eight or ten yards and cut across the field diagonally to receive a forward pass. As the ball arrived, he was hit forcefully with a forearm to the side of his helmet delivered by a linebacker for Team B. The collision resulted in a broken jaw for the receiver. A case could be made that the hit was entirely a clean one, or **sport assertion**. On the other hand, the force and nature of the hit suggested intent to harm, or **instrumental aggression**. A less likely hypothesis, though one with some credibility, was that the linebacker meant to do harm with the goal to harm, or **hostile aggression**. Many plays in contact sports contain elements of all three of these behaviors and making distinctions among them isn't always easy.

As you analyse isolated events in sports, the lines of distinction among the three behaviors above can be indistinct. There are, no doubt, points of overlap among the three conditions, where it's difficult to know just exactly where a particular forceful act falls. For instance, a vicious tackle in football can be nothing more than sport assertion, which is a key ingredient of that very American and violent sport.

One of the more recent controversies in football is players spearing opponents with their helmets. The National Football League has cracked down on helmet to helmet contact, fearing concussions and more serious brain and neck injuries. The league clearly sees this kind of contact as hostile aggression. Some of the players, on the other hand, see rough play as part and parcel of the game, and view their roughness as nothing more than sport assertion: that is, no intent to harm accompanied by liberal use of energy and force.

Theories of aggression

In an effort to better understand aggression, theorists have come up with at least six possible explanations. One of them is **genetic**. Can aggression be an inherited trait? One avenue of research in this area involves the XYY chromosomal make-up. The theory assumes that males are inherently more aggressive than females (which may or may not be true) and since the Y chromosome is male, individuals with two Y chromosomes are born with a double dose of potential for aggression. Research has not supported this area of inquiry.

Another explanation is **hormonal**, with much emphasis here on the male hormone, testosterone. Males are generally observed to be more aggressive than females, and the theory places the blame on the abundance of testosterone males carry around in their chemical make-up.

A third theory is **neurological**, focusing on the effects of brain tumors and other brain abnormalities on behavior.

Herbert Spencer has provided us with a fourth theory, based on his **survival of the fittest** hypothesis. Interestingly, this theory has often been used to explain the supposed superiority of black athletes. The assumption is that only the physically fittest of the slaves survived the cruel trip from Africa and subsequent slavery, thus paying little attention to cunning and guile as survival skills.

The final theories that have the most proponents are the **cathartic theory** and the **social learning** position. The catharsis position assumes that engaging in aggression is cathartic (i.e. it purges the individual of aggressive impulses) and thus reduces the likelihood of its later recurrence. On the other hand, the social learning people suggest that getting away with or watching someone else succeed with aggression only serves to reinforce it. We saw in Chapter 2 that reinforcement by definition increases the likelihood of a behavior occurring again, and that is the focus of the social learning position.

Sports analysts of all persuasions in the US have argued the merits of the two philosophical positions, using the unusually violent sport of football, especially the professional variety, to make their points. Those endorsing the catharsis theory would have us believe that providing a socially acceptable forum for the expression of aggression (i.e. the football field) reduces its expression off the field. The social learning position would be that aggression reinforced on the football field would be likely to generalize to life situations external to football, thus making aggression against others more likely.

 THINK ABOUT IT The famous incident that took place in the 2006 soccer World Cup in which French captain Zinedine Zidane headbutted Marco Materazzi comes to mind here. Zidane apparently lost his composure over some off-the-field comments Materazzi had made earlier, but there's no evidence that the aggressive acts carried over into Zidane's personal life. Apparently the act, though not to be condoned, exerted a cathartic effect on Zidane that was confined to the soccer pitch.

FAQ **Q.** I'm interested in learning more about aggression related to American football. It seems to be rampant and I was wondering if there was something I could read that would enlighten me on the subject.

A. Jeff Benedict and Don Yaeger published a book in 1998 titled *Pros and Cons: The Criminals who Play in the NFL*. These authors studied the records of 509 NFL players from the 1996–97 season and found that 109, or 21%, had been arrested one or more times for crimes ranging from murder (two cases) to rape (seven), domestic violence (45), and assault and battery (42). Benedict has also written two other books on aggression among professional athletes: *Out of Bounds: Inside the NBA's Culture of Rape, Violence, and Crime*, and *Public Heroes, Private Felons*.

Physical factors and aggression

Another method used to explain sport aggression concerns physical factors such as **temperature**, **noise**, and **crowding**. It's generally thought that temperature and aggression go together in a linear fashion – that is, as temperature rises, so does aggression. The research seems to point to an optimal temperature for aggression to take place, with extremes at either end of the scale inhibiting aggression. With regard to noise and crowding, they are understudied and it's probably best to view them not as causes of aggression but more as facilitators once it's expressed.

Psychological factors and aggression

Aggression may be fostered or promoted by such psychological factors as vicarious reinforcement, modeling, and direct external rewards. Essentially **vicarious reinforcement** refers to the tendency to repeat behaviors for which we see others getting rewarded. The effects of vicarious reinforcement are tempered by **modeling**: the greater the similarity between the model and the youth athlete, the greater the likelihood of the observed behavior (or misbehavior) being repeated. Thus, it's important that these identifications be with positive behavior rather than negative. Seeing a rugby union player get rewarded for putting an opponent out of a game with a high tackle or for eye-gouging in the scrum is not what we want our youth to emulate.

As for **direct external rewards**, we are talking about a number of reinforcers in the external world that might foster aggression:

- One of these external reinforcers is highly tangible and something we can all identify with: **money**.

- Another is **status** or respect among one's peers. Having a nickname such as The Enforcer, Dr Death, or The Assassin confers a certain amount of status to people in sports where assertiveness and aggression abound, such as American football.

- A third reinforcement has to do with the **infliction of injury** on an opponent. Hopefully, athletes who identify with this source of reward are few.

- The final external reinforcer is **avoiding negative treatment** by the coach through the infliction of pain on others. The eye-for-an-eye mentality of a professional ice hockey game comes to mind here. Beating up on each other to avoid the wrath of one's peers, coaches, management, or the fans is commonplace in hockey. The comedian Rodney Dangerfield summed up aggression in hockey well: 'I once went to a boxing match and a hockey game broke out!'

 The sport of boxing represents a real ethical enigma for the sport psychologist. The avowed purpose of boxing is to engage in hostile aggression and the infliction of pain. Sport psychologists have shied away from working with boxers because of their clear intent to do harm for harm's sake. The following quote from an unnamed boxer hammers home the problem sport psychologists have with assisting boxers to become more proficient in their sport: 'I don't want to knock him out. I want to hit him, step away and watch him hurt. I want his heart.' Contrast this position with that of perhaps the greatest boxer of the era, Manny Pacquaio of the Philippines. His philosophy is be smart, work hard, enjoy your sport, and be nice to opponents outside the ring. Pacquaio is practising Catholic, a Congressman in his home country's government, and a goodwill ambassador for boxing. For the boxers who might be reading this book, how do your motivations match up with the two contrasting positions expressed here?

Sociological factors

An interesting sociological phenomenon is **hooliganism**, that quintessential gang behavior most often associated with soccer in the UK. It seems that the word 'hooliganism' was first used in a police report in London in 1898, though it's not clear where the term originated. One theory is that it refers to an Irish street hoodlum named Patrick Hooligan. Another is that it came from an Irish street gang named Hooley, and a third is that it's tied to the Irish word 'hooley', which means a wild, spirited party. Irrespective of its origin, hooliganism is pretty much now associated with fan misbehavior in European soccer. The violence of hooligans is fueled greatly by alcohol and is directed at players, officials, and, more often than not, rival gangs. Darts, beer cans, coins, and petrol bombs have all been used as weapons. They often turn the soccer field into a battlefield.

The role of the **media** as a sociological phenomenon in aggression is a sticky wicket. There are many who suggest that the biggest corruptive force in modern Western society is television and, to a lesser extent, the other media. They are convinced that the daily diet of violence seen on television has to promote violence on the part of the viewers, particularly the young. Opposing views suggest that the effects aren't nearly as dramatic as that, and the variables that might contribute to violence are innumerable and hard to control in scientific studies. While there are sports-related studies suggesting that fan enjoyment is enhanced by roughness of play, the issue is far from resolved.

Curbing sports aggression and violence

If an approach to curbing aggression is to be successful, it must involve players, coaches, management, game officials, and the media.

 First of all, players must assume responsibility for their behavior: aggression, after all, is a choice. When tempers flare, as they will from time to time, be a peacemaker.

Coaches should encourage sportsmanship and minimize hatred. Hating one's opponents is considered acceptable, even admirable, by many coaches, but that doesn't make it right.

As for management, monitoring alcohol sales, promoting sports events as family affairs, dealing swiftly and firmly with fan misbehavior, and monitoring coaches and players who play outside the rules and good sportsmanship are essential.

Game officials can help curb aggression by applying the rules even-handedly and making intelligent use of instant replays to ensure the rules and interpretations are applied uniformly and fairly.

Finally, the media can help by stopping the glorification of violence. Yes, violence sells advertisements and newspaper copies by appealing to the worst in all of us, but it does little for the integrity of sports.

IF YOU REMEMBER ONE THING Aggression is defined as the application of something negative to an unwilling victim with the intent to harm and with an expectancy of success. Aggression is promoted by physical, psychological, and sociological factors.

11. Psychological assessment

Psychological assessment has been around in some form or another for centuries, but it was formalized in 1908 with the creation of the Binet–Simon Test of Intelligence in France. Alfred Binet, a psychologist, and Theodore Simon, a physician, were asked by the French government to create an objective test that could be used to screen educationally unfit children from the school system. In 1916, Dr Lewis Terman, Professor of Psychology at Stanford University, further refined the test and it has been known since then as the Stanford–Binet. The Stanford–Binet has been updated over the years and remains one of the leading individual tests of intelligence.

The Wonderlic Personnel Test

In reality, testing of intelligence has never generated much interest among sport psychologists, with one exception. The Wonderlic Personnel Test is a 50-item measure of general intellectual ability, takes twelve minutes to complete, and has been administered to 125 million people since its creation in 1937. In the 1970s, the National Football League (NFL) became interested in the Wonderlic as part of their never-ending search for clues about the psychological make-up of professional football players. As a result, scores of NFL players are easily accessed via the internet.

CASE STUDY

The latest Wonderlic scores have been published on the internet for all the starting NFL quarterbacks in 2010, the scores ranging from 14 to 48 with an average of 28. We obviously focus a lot on quarterbacks, but what are the average scores for the other positions? Those data have been compiled, and are as follows:

Offensive tackles – 26
Centers – 25
Offensive Guards – 23
Tight Ends – 22
Safeties – 19
Linebackers – 19
Cornerbacks – 18
Wide Receivers – 17
Fullbacks – 16
Running Backs – 16

TRY IT NOW!

Imagine you're an athlete who hopes to play professionally. As part of the selection process, taking a Wonderlic intelligence test is mandatory. To get some idea of what lies ahead, complete the questions below. (These can also be seen at: http://www.angelfire.com/fl3/existence/wonderlic/html)

You have two minutes to answer these nine items. Your score can then be translated to a Wonderlic equivalent. Start now.

1. Look at the row of numbers below. What number should come next?

   8   4   2   1   1/2   1/4   ?

2. Assume the first two statements are true. The boy plays football. All football players wear helmets. The boy wears a helmet. Is the final statement true, false, or not certain?

3. How many of the five pairs of items below are exact duplicates?

Nieman, K.M.	Neiman, K.M.
Thomas, G.K.	Thomas, C.K.
Hoff, J.P.	Hoff, J P.
Pino, L.R.	Pina, L.R.
Warner, T.S.	Wanner, T.S.

4. Reserve/Resent – Do these words

   Have similar meanings?
   Have contradictory meanings?
   Mean neither the same nor opposite?

5. A train travels 20 feet in 1/5 second. At this same speed, how many feet will it travel in 3 seconds?

6. The ninth month of the year is

   October   January   June   September   May

7. Which number in the following group of numbers represents the smallest amount?

   7   .8   2   31   .33

8. The hours of daylight and darkness in SEPTEMBER are nearest equal to the hours of daylight and darkness in:

   June   March   May   November

9. Assume the first two statements are true. Bill greeted Beth. Beth greeted Ben. Bill did not greet Ben.

   True?   False?   Not certain?

Scoring key:	
9 correct = 50	4 correct = 22
8 correct = 44	3 correct = 17
7 correct = 39	2 correct = 11
6 correct = 33	1 correct = 6
5 correct = 27	0 correct = 0

The Wonderlic scores are a continuing source of interest to US sports fans because the scores of carefully selected college football players are published on the internet each year. These scores are obtained from a battery of psychological tests administered at the NFL Combine, where the top collegiate players show off their talents for the coaches and scouts in attendance. Most of the posted scores are those of quarterbacks because of their star status and the widely held belief that their position requires the most intelligence.

There are some serious ethical concerns over the release of these test scores to the general public without player consent. A number of sport psychologists have called for an end to this exercise in voyeurism, and rightly so. It can easily be argued that management has a right to this information for player selection purposes, but there's no good reason why the public should know any of it.

FAQ

Q. The Wonderlic test has been around for 75 years and has been administered to people from all walks of life and occupational specialties. In order to get some idea of where I stand, what are some representative scores from some well-known occupational groups?

A. Average scores for a number of vocational fields have been developed: a sample of chemists averaged 31, followed by attorneys 30, computer programmers 29, news writers 26, sales personnel 24, bank tellers 22, clerical workers 21, security guards 17, and janitors 15.

Types of tests used in sport psychology assessment

Essentially, psychological tests can measure **enduring traits**, **temporary states**, or both in the form of **sport-specific tests**.

Enduring traits

Intelligence is an enduring trait, or one that doesn't change much after early childhood as a result of daily events and stressors. The same can be said for trait anxiety, optimism, mental toughness, and locus of control, all of which have been discussed in other chapters. Scores of personality traits have piqued the interest of sport psychologists, and a number of assessment devices have been used to try to identify those traits that are most related to success in athletics. One popular test that has been used extensively in and beyond sport is the **Eysenck Personality Inventory** (EPI), a measure of neuroticism and introversion–extraversion. One consistent finding from EPI results is that athletes on the whole are extraverts, though long-distance runners tend to be introverts. Another major assessment tool is based on the **Personality Big Five**:

* Openness to new experience

- Conscientiousness
- Extraversion
- Agreeableness
- Neuroticism.

However, the Big Five tests haven't been especially useful in sport psychology, which has led to more of a focus on assessing temporary states or sport-specific traits and states.

Temporary states

Two of the major measures of state anxiety, the **State–Trait Anxiety Inventory** (STAI) and the **Competitive State Anxiety Inventory** (CSAI), were discussed in the chapter on anxiety assessment. However, there's one scale that has received major attention among sport psychologists, and that's the **Profile of Mood States** (POMS). The POMS was created in 1971 as a means of quantifying progress in counseling or psychotherapy, but **Dr William Morgan**, a professor at the University of Wisconsin, introduced the scale to sport psychology by using it with US Olympic athletes in 1972 and 1976. Since that time, the POMS has been used in well over 500 published studies in dozens of sports.

In its original form, the POMS was 65 items long, and measured **tension**, **depression**, **anger**, **vigor**, **fatigue**, and **confusion**. A **total mood disturbance score** can be computed by subtracting the sum of the five negative mood states from the positive dimension of vigor. If the vigor score is high and the other five low, it's possible to get a negative total mood disturbance score, which of course is a good sign. An athlete with a low or minus mood score should be free of crippling emotions that would interfere with good performance. For example, my colleagues and I once tested large numbers of professional female tennis players and one of them, arguably the best player ever, scored a minus 18, the lowest score we have ever seen among literally thousands we have tested over the years. Of late, there have been a number of attempts to reduce the items on the POMS, and one of these that has gained popularity contains 30 items with virtually no loss of reliability or validity.

Q. I'm a senior in college and I hope someday to be a sport psychologist. I'm curious about where I might find solid information about psychological tests that are on the market. Where might I go to find good information?

A. One excellent source of information is always the manual that accompanies almost every test. Another is the *Mental Measurements Yearbook* (MMY), which has been published since 1938. The MMY lists 2,000 published tests by type, provides carefully considered critiques, and cites relevant research so that the user may choose among them more confidently. You might also consult the *Directory of Psychological Tests in the Sport and Exercise Sciences* edited by Dr Andrew Ostrow of the University of

West Virginia, or a volume I edited titled *Bibliography of Psychological Tests Used in Sport and Exercise Psychology Research and Practice.*

Sport-specific tests

A number of instruments have come out in response to calls from practising sport psychologists for tests that have inherent appeal to athletes, or what we call **face validity**. A test that has face validity is one that an athlete can look at and say, 'Hey, these items are related to things I do in my sport every day.' It's one thing to assess personality by asking an athlete how he feels about a walk in the park on a lazy Sunday afternoon, and another to ask how he responds to pressure in the last two or three minutes of a basketball game. The latter clearly has more face validity for the athlete.

One of the earliest and most ambitious attempts to create a sport-specific test took place in 1969 by **Drs Bruce Ogilvie and Thomas Tutko** at San Jose State University in California. Their test was called the **Athletic Motivation Inventory** (AMI), made up of 190 items that attempted to measure:

1. The desire to be successful in athletics.
2. The ability to withstand the emotional stress of competition.
3. Dedication to the sport and the coach.

Their work was well received and the AMI became the instrument of choice for the National Hockey League (NHL) for many years. As a side note, Bruce Ogilvie is generally accorded the title of 'Father of Applied Sport Psychology' for his pioneering work in the field. Ogilvie taught, conducted research, wrote several books and numerous professional articles while also consulting with over 50 professional teams in several sports. I also owe Bruce Ogilvie a debt of gratitude for his mentorship and advice when I was trying to make my entry into the field of sport psychology in 1980 and 1981.

Dr Michael Mahoney and several colleagues created a test in 1987 called the **Psychological Skills Inventory for Sports** (PSIS) which measured six psychological skills they thought were most germane to performance excellence in sports. The test was 45 items long and measured:

- Concentration
- Anxiety management
- Self-confidence
- Mental preparation
- Motivation
- Team emphasis.

The scale was reasonably well-received but subsequent research showed that three of the sub-scales measured things very well and three did not. The PSIS is seldom used in sport psychology today but it did set a tone for other researchers.

An outstanding sport-specific scale available today was published in 1995 in the *Journal of Sport & Exercise Psychology* by **Drs Ronald Smith** and **Frank Smoll** at the University of Washington in Seattle, **Dr Robert Schutz** of the University of British Columbia, and **Dr J.T. Ptacek** of Bucknell University. It's called the **Athletic Coping Skills Inventory** (ACSI), is 28 items in length, and measures seven sub-scales:

- Coping with adversity
- Peaking under pressure
- Goal setting and mental preparation
- Concentration
- Freedom from worry
- Confidence and achievement motivation
- Coachability.

Research using the ACSI suggests that it's a valid measure of sport-related mental skills and it continues to be used a great deal in sport psychology research and practice. Below are the ACSI sub-scales and the character traits applying to each one. You can use them to shed light on your own psychological characteristics as a sportsperson.

TRY IT NOW!

The ACSI sub-scales and items

All items are answered on a four-point scale:

    0 – almost never
    1 – sometimes
    2 – often
    3 – almost always

Coping with adversity

I maintain emotional control no matter how things are going for me.

When things are going badly, I tell myself to keep calm, and this works for me.

When I feel myself getting too tense, I can quickly relax my body and calm myself.

I remain positive and enthusiastic during competition, no matter how badly things are going.

Peaking under pressure

To me, pressure situations are challenges that I welcome.

The more pressure there is during a game, the more I enjoy it.

I tend to play better under pressure because I think more clearly.

I make fewer mistakes when the pressure's on because I can concentrate better.

Goal setting/mental preparation

On a daily or weekly basis, I set very specific goals for myself that guide what I do.

I tend to do lots of planning about how to reach my goals.

I set my own performance goals for each practice.

I have my own game plan worked out in my head long before the game begins.

I set my own performance goals for each practice.

Concentration

I handle unexpected situations in my sport very well.

When I am playing sports, I can focus my attention and block out distractions.

It is easy for me to keep distracting thoughts from interfering with something I am watching or listening to.

It is easy for me to direct my attention and focus on a single subject or person.

Freedom from worry

While competing, I worry about making mistakes or failing to come through.

I put a lot of pressure on myself by worrying how I will perform.

I think about and imagine what will happen if I screw up.

I worry quite a bit about what others think about my performance.

Confidence and achievement motivation

I feel confident I will play well.

I get the most out of my talent and skills.

When I fail to reach my goals, it makes me try even harder.

I don't have to be pushed to practice or play hard; I give 100%.

Coachability

If a coach criticizes or yells at me, I correct the mistake without getting upset about it.

When a coach or manager criticizes me, I become upset rather than helped.

I improve my skills by listening carefully to advice and instruction from coaches and managers.

When a coach or manager tells me how to correct mistakes I've made, I tend to take it personally and feel upset.

To give you some idea of what the scores mean, the following scores were obtained from 1,000 college students at the University of Washington:

Subscale	Males	Females
Coping with adversity	6.37	6.11
Peaking under pressure	6.76	5.91
Goal setting/mental preparation	5.84	4.98
Concentration	7.20	6.78
Freedom from worry	6.32	6.64
Confidence and achievement motivation	8.12	7.50
Coachability	9.25	8.89
Total score	**49.46**	**46.81**

IF YOU REMEMBER ONE THING

Psychological tests can measure enduring traits, temporary states, or sport-specific characteristics.

12. Risk-sport athletes, injured athletes, black athletes

Risk-sport athletes

What is a risk sport? Sports authorities and participants agree that bungee jumping, hang gliding, ice and rock climbing, motorcycle racing, scuba diving, and sky diving are legitimate risk sports. A number of studies have been conducted with risk-sport participants and they appear to be a pretty nondescript group for the most part. For example, one study of hang gliding participants found them to be male, Anglo, mid-twenties, from every walk of life, in love with their subculture, see their sport as risky but not dangerous, and prone to get a rush, or a blast or a high from their experiences. Another study of rock climbers found them to be pretty much average on every measure. Another related study of climbers of the ultimate challenge, Mount Everest, found a rather remarkable group of athletes, ranging from several talented and nationally ranked skiers to a couple of college football players to a nationally ranked motocross racer.

Correlates of high risk-sport participation

Two strong predictors of participation in risk sports have been strongly supported by psychological research, one of which is **birth order**. Several studies have noted a disproportionate number of participants who were second, third, or fourth born in the family sequence. The explanation for this may be that first-borns find their rewards in more traditional arenas such as academics and sports such as football, baseball, soccer, or basketball. On the other hand, later-borns seek the spotlight by challenging death on the slopes, in the seas, or through the airways.

A second predictor is **sensation seeking**, a psychological concept popularized by Dr Marvin Zuckerman, who suggests that risk sports participants are sensation seekers, or people who like to live on the edge. Zuckerman has created a scale to measure this trait, called the **Sensation-Seeking Scale** (SSS) which has four sub-components:

- **Thrill and Adventure Seeking** (TAS): the desire to engage in thrill seeking, risk, and adventurous activities such as parachuting, hang gliding, mountain climbing, and so on
- **Experience Seeking** (ES): seeking arousal through mind, sense, and non-conforming lifestyle
- **Disinhibition** (Dis): release through partying, drinking, gambling, and sex, generally regarded as more traditional sensation-seeking outlets
- **Boredom Susceptibility** (BS): aversion to repetition, routine, and boring people; restlessness when escape from tedium is not possible.

The SSS has been used successfully with a number of different athletic groups. For example, Dr William Straub of

Ithaca College in New York compared hang gliders, automobile racers, and bowlers on the SSS. As might be expected, when compared to the other two risk activities, the bowlers were lower on the total sensation seeking score and two of the four sub-scales. Straub also asked a simple question to the effect of, 'Do you think of your sport as a risk activity?' 67% of the hang gliders and 50% of the auto racers said yes to the question, but none of the bowlers saw their sport as risky, again unsurprisingly.

THINK ABOUT IT

Scoring the Sensation Seeking Scale
To arrive at scores for the SSS, Zuckerman asks respondents to answer 64 questions on whether or not they have done things of a risk nature. Then, respondents are asked to answer the same questions regarding their intentions for the future. Examples include:

Climbing steep mountains
Reading books about explicit sex
Going to a wild, uninhibited party
Having premarital sexual relations
Taking an unknown drug
Horseback riding at a gallop
Discussing your sex life with your friends
Exploring caves
'Doing what feels good' regardless of the consequences
Nude swimming in the company of persons of both sexes

You can find out where you stand on sensation seeking by taking a short test posted on the following website: http://www.bbc.co.uk/science/humanbody/mind/sensation

Injured athletes

Injuries are part and parcel of sports participation at every level. Literally, there will be millions of sports injuries every year, ranging in degree from mild to severe, and encompassing the informal games and sports on the playground all the way to the professional level. Strains, sprains, inflammations, pulls, tears, bruises, bumps, and concussions are an integral part of the everyday experience of the athlete, sports trainer, and sports medicine practitioner. As one goes up the hierarchy from informal sports to youth sports to the professional level, the injuries become more common and more severe.

A prominent European cyclist once gave me his impressions of injuries in professional soccer and cycling. He said that cyclists often fall and are subject to fractures, strains, sprains, and contusions, none of which are too likely to evolve into lifetime infirmities. On the other hand, he said that he had many friends who had retired from the highest level of professional soccer in Germany, and none could walk by the time they were 40 or 45 years of age. He was exaggerating to make his point, of course, but was referring to the many ankle and knee injuries that are so much a part of the life of the professional soccer player. It's difficult to play that sport for 20 or 30 years and not show considerable wear and tear on the connective tissue in the leg joints.

Other sports with reputations for leg injuries include basketball, American football, and rugby. Hand, wrist, elbow, and back injuries are the bane of golfers and tennis players, and inflammation or tissue damage to the rotator cuff are common to bowlers in cricket. And how many major league baseball pitchers have experienced 'Tommy John surgery', so-named for the player whose own surgical repair opened the door for the career-saving procedure that is now commonplace in the repairing of injured elbows? Clearly, there are significant risks associated with big-time sports participation. Whether or not they can be predicted from a psychological point of view is a tough question.

Predicting sports injuries

Predicting sports injuries is a difficult proposition that must take into account psychological variables, situational events, the history of personal stressors, and one's coping resources. **Psychologically**, hardiness, locus of control, self-concept, competitive anxiety, Type A personality, and mood states have all received some attention from researchers.

Intuitively, it would follow that people who are psychologically tough (i.e. hardy), in a positive mood state, and with a healthy self-concept would be at lower risk for injury. The available research is slightly supportive of this conclusion, but more work needs to be done.

Research on the hard-charging, aggressive Type A personality has shown a positive relationship between the personality disposition and sports injury in distance runners: that is, the more Type-A the person is, the more frequently he or she will suffer an injury while training or competing. Having an external or internal locus of control seems to be unrelated to injury, suggesting that this personality variable has little or nothing to do with predicting sports injuries.

The **stresses** associated with life events and daily hassles might be of more relevance in understanding sports injuries. For example, several pieces of research looking at life stresses such as death in the family, serious economic setbacks, and divorce have consistently supported a relationship between these types of events and susceptibility to both injury and psychosomatic illness. This relationship has been supported in studies involving alpine skiing, figure skating, American football, gymnastics, soccer, and wrestling.

Coping resources that might bear on the injury relationship include the athlete's social support network as well as his or her own repertoire of coping behaviors such as those suggested in Chapters 4, 5, and 6.

Recovering from Injury

Athletes, particularly male ones, are told from Day One in their sport experience to not give in to pain or injury for fear of losing their playing position or appearing to be a wimp – that would be a violation of the macho code that permeates sport. A 'no pain, no gain', 'no blood, no foul' approach to injury prevails at all levels. And coaches and over-zealous parents are partners in crime in creating and promoting this mentality.

The macho code notwithstanding, what can be done to get an injured athlete rehabilitated and back on his or her feet? One strategy is **goal setting**, where realistic and achievable goals for recovery are formulated and put into practice. Another approach discussed earlier is **positive self-talk**. A third technique with potential is **visualization**, where healing imagery can be most effective in speeding recovery.

Countering negative thoughts with positive self-talk

Negative thought

'I'll probably always limp on this bad leg.'

'It looks like my muscles are atrophying.'

Positive replacement

'I can whip this injury with hard work.'

'My leg is getting stronger every day.'

Negative thought	Positive replacement
'I may never recover from this injury.'	'I will get better as I am a fast healer.'
'I'm not sure my doctor knew what he was doing. Maybe someone else could have done a better job on my knee.'	'I'm going to fool my doctor and get better a lot faster than he predicted.'

Black athletes

Most of the discussion about minorities in sport has focused on the black athlete, and space limitations will unfortunately prevent us from looking into other important under-represented minority groups. A modicum of scientific information is available concerning black athletes, but superstition and misinformation abound. One incorrect belief is that black athletes dominate sports across the board. In the US, the high-profile sports of college and professional football, college and professional basketball, track and field, and boxing are certainly dominated by black athletes. On the other hand, sports such as bowling, golf, hockey, rugby, swimming, tennis, and volleyball are almost entirely the province of white athletes. Two other prominent sports, baseball and soccer, are predominantly white but are quite mixed racially overall.

A common misconception is that black athletes dominate because they survived the horrors of the slave ships that brought them from Africa to what is now the US and the Caribbean 400 years ago. This notion assumes that physical superiority allowed the slaves to survive. This same 'survival of the fittest' argument is then extrapolated to explain black dominance in sports. In this regard, Jon Entine, an oft-quoted authority on sports and race, says: 'The racist stereotype of the "animalistic black" stretches back centuries. Fascination about black physicality and black anger about being caricatured as a lesser human being, closer to being a jungle beast, has been a part of the dark side of the American dialogue on race ...' However, nowhere does intelligence and guile get factored into the survival equation. It's probably safe to assume that many survived the slave-ship horrors and subsequent slavery itself not because they were necessarily physically superior but because they were smart (or perhaps 'street smart'). But old racial stereotypes die hard.

One of the more interesting slants on the black athlete comes from work conducted from the 1970s to the 1990s concerning the tendency of coaches and athletic administrators to assign white or Anglo athletes to central (i.e. 'thinking')

positions and blacks to peripheral, or reactive positions requiring considerable athletic ability and not much else.

This positioning by race was known as the **sport opportunity structure**, and **stacking** was the practice that arose from it. Thus, stacking in American football had Anglos occupy the center, quarterback, and kicker positions and blacks the wide receiver, running back, and defensive back slots. In basketball, stacking mandated that point guards be white because they had to 'quarterback' the team. Typically, centers were white but shooting guards and forwards black, because athleticism as opposed to intelligence is a prime requisite for these positions. In baseball, the catcher, pitcher, shortstop, second base, and the centerfield position were all white, and blacks filled first base, third base, and the other two outfield positions.

Even today in baseball, it's not at all unusual to find that the first base coach is black and the third base coach Anglo. Essentially, all the first base coach does is congratulate a player when he gets a hit, take the protective equipment he used when batting, and tell him to not get doubled off of first base by a line drive. At third base, however, one has to think. Critical decisions about who should try to score and who should not are high-level intellectual undertakings, at least if you're looking at the issue from a stacking frame of mind.

Racism in the US softened in the 1980s and 1990s, thus creating an environment that allowed black athletes to thrive in sports at all levels. With it went most of the practice of stacking. However, critics contend that there are still vestiges of racism and stacking, particularly at the management level in sports. Major sports organizations world-wide are largely the domain of white administrators and, to a large extent, white coaches. Hopefully, as racism continues to diminish, so will the last remnants of stacking.

THINK ABOUT IT

How many of you older readers have heard the racist-based litany that 'you can't win with a black quarterback'? The racist assumption behind this statement is that intelligence and calmness under fire are required, and the black athlete is not a thinker and an agent of calm. Rather, they are athletic, impulsive, high-strung, and so on, but definitely not thinkers under pressure. An interesting transformation has taken place over the past two decades, and the racist litany has been replaced now by a reverse racist sentiment to the effect that 'you can't win if you have a white quarterback'.

A second take on black athletic superiority rests on genetic explanations: simply put, blacks are genetically endowed to excel in athletics. In the words of Isiah Thomas, the NBA Hall of Fame basketball player:

When whites perform well, it's due to their thinking and work habit. It's not the case for blacks. All we do is run and jump. We never practice or give a thought to how we play. It's like I came dribbling out of my mother's womb.

However, there are some problems associated with this argument, one of which is the issue of what is a black. Hundreds of years of sexual relations between Anglos and blacks, blacks and Hispanics, and combinations of all of those racial groups have led to a pretty nebulous definition of 'black'. A second problem with a genetic explanation is that most of the evidence for black superiority is anecdotal and based on studies and observations of only exceptional athletes. Blacks with average, low, or no athletic ability are seldom if ever part of the equation. A third problem is that there are probably more differences *within* the races than there are between them. We have all seen blacks and whites who couldn't walk and chew gum at the same time, and we have seen the gifted ones at the other end of the spectrum also. Finally, while people are quick to jump on the genetics bandwagon in explaining black superiority, they never talk of a judo gene to explain Japanese domination of that sport. Nor is there so much as a whisper about the Swiss or Scandinavian skiing gene that allows them to dominate the slopes. And when was the last time you heard of a Bulgarian weightlifting gene? Or a Sri Lankan cricket gene? How about a Canadian or Russian hockey gene? Or try a volleyball gene to explain why Californian men and women dominate that sport in the US? Clearly, geography, opportunity, and historical background have much to do with excellence, thus weakening the genetic position.

 We have talked of black domination of sports, particularly the male sports of football and boxing. Does this same picture exist for black female collegiate athletes in the US? Dr Emmett Gill, a professor of sociology at Rutgers University, asserts that this is an illusion. He cites the following statistics to back up his points:

- Black female participation in college sports has grown by nine-fold since 1972. 66% of black athletes graduate from college compared to 50% of black female non-athletes.
- 90% of black female athletes compete in two sports, basketball and track and field.
- Black females make up less than 5% of all female collegiate athletes.
- In women's lacrosse, rowing, and soccer, Anglo athletes outnumber blacks 11,692 to 594.
- A woman's field hockey player is 64 times more likely to be Anglo than black; in swimming, the figure is 60 times more likely; and in rowing it's 44 times more likely.
- To achieve parity with Anglos, it would take 347 black females in soccer, 434 in swimming, and 429 in rowing.

Black dominance in the sprints and distance events

There's no question that black athletes are over-represented in some sports, and nowhere is this more apparent than in the sprints and distance events in athletics. For example, Jon Entine reports that all 32 of the finalists in the 100-meter dash during the past four summer Olympic games, and 797 of the top 800 times in the history of the 100-meter dash, have been posted by sprinters of West African descent. The statistical likelihood of this occurring by chance, according to Entine, is 0.000000000000000000000000000001.

As for the distance events, men from Kenya hold world records in the 3,000-meter race, the 15-, 20-, and 25-kilometer road races, the half marathon, and the marathon. Kenyan women own half of the top ten times in the marathon and world records in the 10-, 20-, and 25-kilometer races. These records are made even more remarkable when one considers that they are from a single tribe called the Kalenjin residing in one area of Kenya with only 3 million people.

 High-risk sports participants, injured athletes, and black athletes are of considerable interest to sport scientists. Participation in risk sports is at an all-time high, injured athletes are being assisted with recovery through physical and psychological strategies, and controversies and misinformation abound surrounding the emergence of the black athlete over the past half-century.

13. Youth sport

If you can meet with triumph and disaster
And treat those two imposters just the same ...
You'll be a man my son! [or a fine young woman]
Rudyard Kipling in his classic poem, 'If'

There are few places in the world where children are not involved in sports at some level or another. Probably a runaway in terms of overall global popularity would be football (soccer), where little equipment is needed and almost any open spot in a vacant lot can become a pitch. Highly organized soccer development programs begin early in most of the world. As one example, nearly 5 million German male and female youths between the ages of 7 and 14 have begun formalized training from soccer agencies in that country. Similar programs can be found in most other countries, even in those that are less developed and industrialized.

In the US, perhaps as many as 48 million young people between the ages of 5 and 18 take part in organized sport. Particularly popular sports at the high school level are basketball, American football, soccer, and track and field (i.e. athletics) for boys, and basketball, soccer, softball, track and field, and volleyball for girls. Unfortunately, sports have been transformed over time into a pressure-cooker environment that strips much of the fun from participation for many young people.

It's this quest for fun coupled with the unfortunate tendency for parents and coaches to make sports so dreadful for some young people that has prompted sport psychologists to take a closer look at youth sport. For example, a number of training packages have been created to enhance the quality of coaching at the youth level.

 A leader in improving the quality of coaching is Dr Ronald Smith and his colleagues at the University of Washington in Seattle. The group has focused their research on youth sport coaching, particularly with baseball, and a program known as **Coach Effectiveness Training** (CET) has emerged from their efforts.

In many cases, youth sport coaches have played the sport they are coaching, but they lack an understanding of the needs of children. As well, they often have no idea how to deal with the parents of their players. CET effectively addresses these issues by providing instruction on the proper use of positive reinforcement, the occasional use of punishment, technical instruction, and organizational and communication skills training.

Smith and his colleagues have trained many parent volunteers, and when coaches who have taken part in their training are compared with those who have not done so, several interesting results emerge. In general, there are often no differences in the winning and losing percentages among the two groups of coaches, but players of coaches who have received the CET training report that they like their sports more, are more favorably disposed toward their coaches, and express greater enjoyment of what they are doing than do kids who play for the untrained coaches.

Product versus process orientation to sport

One way sport psychologists think about youth sports is to apply a framework that emphasizes a **product** versus **process** orientation.

In the product orientation, winning matters above all else, competition is made more meaningful if there is some kind of external reward or prize involved, the game is played more for the admiration of others than the pure joy of participating, and domination, and in some cases dehumanization, of the opponent is of extreme importance.

On the other hand, the process orientation believes that winning isn't an end in itself, striving for personal and team excellence are highly sought after goals, harmony, one-ness, rhythm, and aesthetic appreciation are integral parts of competition, and rapport with opponents, not domination, is a vital part of excellence in personal and team performance. The opposing player is seen as a valued ally, not an enemy, for without him or her there would be no competition.

Where do you stand on this issue as a player or coach: do you endorse the process or worship the product?

Why do kids take part in sports?

Roughly twenty years ago, the Athletic Footwear Association (AFA) conducted an intensive study of youth sport participation motives, as well as reasons for dropping out. Eleven cities across the US were carefully selected to yield a representative sample, and responses of 10,000 young people aged 10 through 18 were used for data analysis. Essentially, the study supported results gleaned from a number of earlier studies, indicating that:

1. Sports participation declined steadily from age 10 to 18; 45% of youngsters age 10 took part in sport, whereas only 26% of 18-year-olds did. 'Not having fun' and 'poor coaching' were often cited as major reasons why kids dropped out.

2. Though a somewhat nebulous concept, 'fun' was the main reason for being in a sport, and lack of fun the main reason for dropping out.

3. Winning was a low priority among young sports participants, and every study of youth sport participation supports this finding.

4. The reasons for participating vary from athlete to athlete, including the most elite performers.

Anxiety in youth sport

Over-zealous parents, well-meaning peers, overly-demanding coaches, and the ever-increasing emphasis on sport specialization at an early age have greatly ratcheted up the pressure on young people who participate in sports. One of the first and most interesting studies of stress in sports was conducted by Dr Rainer Martens at the University of Illinois in the late 1970s. Using the Sport Competition Anxiety Test (SCAT), Martens demonstrated that various sports produce differing effects on pre-adolescent youth. He looked at such sports as American football, ice hockey, baseball, swimming, basketball, gymnastics, and wrestling and found them to produce anxiety levels in the order presented above, with gymnastics and wrestling being the most anxiety-producing.

Subsequent psychological research on anxiety in sport has isolated four major sources of stress.

One of these stressors is how the athlete sees himself or herself athletically. Being selected first (or last) in any game on the playground provides a lot of feedback concerning where one stands athletically.

A second consideration is whether the athlete expects to win or lose; children high in anxiety may feel that they are as talented as their peers but still expect to experience less success in their sport endeavors.

Being negatively evaluated – or better yet, *expecting* to be seen in a negative light by peers or coaches – also serves as a major stressor for youth.

Finally, experiencing negative emotions related to one's sport performance can be detrimental; children high in anxiety seem to experience much more negative emotions than do their peers who are low on anxiety when they perform equally well or equally poorly.

Are you a 'helicopter' parent?

The media occasionally make reference to 'helicopter' parents who hover over every move their children make, and no doubt these parents raise the stress levels of their youth athletes. Look at the characteristics below and see how many apply to you.

- Helicopter parents second-guess and offer inane suggestions to the coaches;
- they try to make sure their children never experience the agony of defeat or the psychic pain associated with failure;
- they wrap their own identity and self-worth around the athletic accomplishments of their children;
- they fight their children's battles for them;
- and they always start conversations about their children's sport experiences with 'We', as in 'We are going to try out for the club rugby team.'

The implicit message conveyed is that the child is weak, incapable, helpless, fragile, and dependent.

Putting the fun back in youth sports

According to Dr Darrell Barnett in his book *Gatorade's Playbook for Kids*, to put the fun back in to children's sports we might begin with some friendly admonitions for parents attending youth sport events. He questioned a number of children about what they would ask of their parents in terms of expected behavior at their games. How many of these have you violated while watching youth sports?

1. Don't yell out instructions;
2. Don't put down the officials;
3. Don't put me down in public;
4. Don't yell at my coach;
5. Don't put down my team-mates;
6. Don't put down the other team;
7. Don't lose your cool;
8. Don't lecture me after the game (one child, referring to the ride home with his father after a game, called it 'the longest fifteen minutes of my life');
9. Don't forget to laugh and have fun;
10. Don't forget it's just a game.

Who has the worst sports parents?

If it hadn't been for sports, I wouldn't have grown up hating my father.

New York executive

IPSOS, a marketing research company, in conjunction with Reuters, surveyed 23,000 adults in 22 countries about the extent to which they had witnessed unsavory behavior at sporting events. People living in the US (60%) were the most likely to have observed unacceptable behavior on the part of parents at a youth sports event, followed by India (59%), Italy (55%), Argentina (54%), Canada (53%), and Australia (50%). The countries least likely to have these experiences were Hungary, the Czech Republic, Mexico, Japan, and France. The coordinator of the study for IPSOS suggests that the country that prides itself most in terms of being civilized, namely the US, seems to be witness to the highest number of uncivilized acts at youth sporting events.

Current status of youth sports

Youth sports have spun out of control in many respects over the past decade or two, especially in the pressure-cooker existence that is the United States. Increasingly, young people are being forced into premature sport specialization because of the pressure to earn a college scholarship or sign a lucrative contract with a professional team in one of the high-profile sports. In the process, much of the fun has been stripped from participating. And fan misbehavior and violence can't be too far behind when the pressure mounts. Headlines such as the following are abundant in the print media:

Umpires say sports for kids becoming brawl games

Losing season prompts dad to sue son's coach

Hockey dad indicted in assault on kid's coach

Sports crazed kids: Year round play. Summer clinics. Pushy parents. Is this too much of a good thing?

Emphasis on winning insidious

These kinds of headlines are proof positive that something has gone awry in youth sports. Whatever happened to the obviously outdated notion that sports ought to be about having fun in the context of good sportsmanship?

 Youth sports participation is at an all-time high, world-wide, and the reasons why kids partici-pate and drop out are numerous and complex. Fun is the number one motive for participating, and win-ning is of secondary importance. There are many sources of anxiety associated with youth sports, not the least of which is out-of-control parents.

---

14. Women in sport

Sarah, a collegiate tennis player, hits the ball with considerable force accompanied by a loud grunt each time she strikes it across the net at her opponent. The loud grunt is met with various degrees of acceptance by people in the crowd. There are those who see this behavior as quite acceptable for a female, indicating a strong desire to compete and win. There are others, perhaps more of the tennis purist variety, who are convinced that such histrionics are 'unladylike' and unbecoming of a female. What do you think about this situation?

The field of psychology is strongly committed to the concept of equality by race, gender, and sexual preference, and this dedication is shared by sport psychologists. The field has many advocates whose major life work is advancing the cause of women who participate in sports and fitness activities. One extremely dedicated force is the Tucker Center for Research on Girls and Women in Sport headquartered at the University of Minnesota in Minneapolis. The center is directed by Dr Mary Jo Kane and serves as a national think-tank for sport scientists with an interest in the female sport and fitness experience.

A brief history

One of the issues confronting female athletes has always been where they fit into the total picture with regard to masculinity and femininity.

In the ancient Olympics which began in Olympia, Greece, in 776 BC, women weren't allowed to participate in or watch the events, on pain of death. However, there was a separate competition for women that began, according to the best estimates of sport historians, somewhere between 800 and 500 BC. This was known as the Heraean games, named in honor of the goddess Hera who was the wife of Zeus, king of the gods, god of the sky and thunder, and ruler of Mount Olympus in Greek mythology. Pausanias, a prominent Greek of that period, describes the Heraean games as follows:

The games consisted of footraces for maidens. They ran in the following way: Their hair hangs down, a tunic reaches to a little above the knee, and they bare a shoulder as far as the breast. These too have the Olympic stadium reserved for their games, but the course of the stadium is shortened for them by about one-sixth of its length. To the winning maidens they give a crown of olives and a portion of the cow sacrificed to Hera.

There is a suggestion that women should be viewed both as sexual objects (the nearly bared breast) and as the weaker sex (the shorter course). Proponents of women's sports have had to contend with this image of sexuality and physical inferiority right up to the present.

The major force behind the creation of the modern Olympics in 1896 was a French nobleman, Baron Pierre de Coubertin, and like his predecessors in ancient Greece, he was adamantly opposed to women participating in the competitions. But tennis and golf were created for women four years later in the 1900 Olympics, and now 35% to 40% of the summer Olympic competitors are women.

Issues related to female participation in sport

Women who participate in sport are constantly confronted with perplexing issues including homophobic challenges to their femininity, the specter of eating disorders, and minimal or distorted coverage of their accomplishments by the media. Let's look at each of these.

Homophobia

As women emerged on the sport and physical education scenes in the mid-1900s, homophobia (the fear or hatred of homosexual individuals) became a pronounced social phenomenon and women were routinely accused of being outside the boundaries of traditional gender roles. Much discussion focused on 'mannish' females in sports and in physical education departments, and terms like 'sweaty lesbian', 'dyke', 'butch' and 'jock' were often applied to female athletes who in some way deviated from the norm in appearance or behavior.

These perceptions were heightened by the emergence of women from the Soviet bloc countries who appeared at world competitions in the 1970s and 80s with flat chests, thin moustaches, and deep voices, features closely associated with the drug doping they were engaging in, with full support (and in too many instances coercion) from their governments. A poignant example of the doping that went on, as well as the blatant disregard for the long-term health of the athletes, was the East German women's swimming teams in the 1970s. The East German women won very few medals in the 1972 Olympics but came back to win virtually every gold medal in 1976, and pretty much with the same swimmers. Those women were testimony to the powers of doping as a means of enhancing performance, and to the political agenda of their government.

Today, there seems to be a much more accepting environment for gay athletes, thanks to changes in the way society looks at homosexuality in general and educational efforts launched by assorted gay and lesbian rights groups.

Eating disorders

Society's fascination with the idea that 'thin is in' has created an environment in which females become preoccupied with their weight and appearance. This fascination can sometimes lead to eating disorders, the best-known of which are **anorexia**, or restricted food intake, and **bulimia**, or excessive food intake. Of the two, the more common and probably more life-threatening is anorexia, which is largely a disorder of adolescence and young adulthood and carries with it a 2–5% mortality rate in extreme cases.

KEY TERM

In the sports world, dieticians, sports medicine physicians, and sport psychologists talk of the **female athletic triad** made up of disordered eating, amenorrhea, and osteoporosis. An athlete may possess one, two, or all three of these conditions, and diagnosis is much more reliable when all three are present. Amenorrhea, or disturbed menstrual functioning, is considered to be the classic warning sign for the disorder, but other prominent symptoms include lanugo (soft, downy body hair); bone anomalies; eroded dental enamel often due to vomiting, which is a part of the obsession with weight and body image management; and compulsive exercise, which is also a deterrent to weight gain. If one calculates how many calories are taken in each day and then gauges exercise to use up all those calories, the result is weight management driven by questionable motives.

Though males in some sports may engage in disordered eating practices, especially those where weight gain or loss is such a focus (e.g. wrestling or horse-racing), the disorder is most prominent among females, especially those in gymnastics, cross country, swimming, and distance running.

Unfortunately, coaches and even athletic trainers are often poorly prepared to detect the warning signs of anorexia, and even more helpless in some cases to work with anorexic athletes. There have been reports of coaches who couldn't name all three legs of the athletic triad, and others who thought that amenorrhea was due to excessive exercise as opposed to disordered eating practices. There have also been studies indicating that as many as 25% of American university athletic departments had no policy on handling eating disorders.

Calculating your Body Mass Index (BMI)

One manifestation of the 'thin is in' movement is seen in non-athlete women such as models and actors. So much emphasis is placed on these women to be rail-thin that it's no wonder they are prone to engage in disordered eating. In an attempt to define and combat this problem, some contests and modeling events have imposed an acceptable **Body Mass Index** (BMI) for all participants. The World Health Organization has created standards for determining this index, with a BMI of 40 considered to be morbidly obese, 30 to 40 obese, 18.5 to 25 ideal, 18.5 underweight, 17.5 anorexic, and 15 indicating starvation.

If you would like to calculate your BMI, there are websites to help you with the calculations. For example, try: http://www.nhblisupport.com/bmi/

Media coverage of female athletes

The world of sports has long been dominated by the **male hegemony**, or the 'good old boy' network of men who call the shots at the management level. One obvious area of male hegemony is in the serious lack of media coverage of female athletes. Study after study shows a substantial under-representation of women in the print media, television, university sports media guides, and other sources. The following data have emerged concerning newspaper coverage:

1. Stories devoted to male athletes outnumber those on females by almost 25 to 1.
2. Over 90% of all sports photographs involve male athletes.
3. Front-page stories devoted to male athletes outnumber those for females by a margin of 4 to 1.
4. As more women participate in sports, the under-representation seems even more disproportional.

A recent media study conducted by the Center for Gender Equality in Iceland, involving both the print media and television, and focusing on sports reports from Austria, Lithuania, Italy, Norway, and Iceland, supported the studies from the US. Men dominated numerically, were more often quoted in stories, were almost always the reporters doing the interviewing, and were more often the focus with regard to their views on sports and their personal lives. This idolization was a two-edged sword for males, for often there was a negative or more sensational aspect to the reports of their personal lives.

Other reports have shown women more often portrayed on their knees in defeat, crying over performance, and generally in positions of weakness. The hint of soft pornography is pervasive, and is the source of constant consternation for those who would like to see traditional gender roles challenged in modern sports reporting. The ultimate in this exploitation of women may well be the annual *Sports Illustrated* swimsuit issue, which has been labeled by one reader as an 'annual exercise in hit and run sexual harassment'.

Psychological studies of females in sport

Of course, it follows that the female sport experience would be of considerable interest to sport psychologists, and this is certainly the case. Research has been plentiful, but we'll look specifically at three areas that demonstrate the evolution of women in sports and society over the past 40 years: **fear of success**, **psychological androgyny**, and sports **attribution theory**.

Fear of success

This is an area that clearly demonstrates the evolution of women in the last 40 years, from a time of timidity and non-assertiveness to one of forcefulness and self-assertion.

CASE STUDY

An American psychologist, Matina Horner, devised some scenarios in the late 1960s and early 70s in which she tested the proposition that women fear success in competitive situations. Essentially, she asked male and female college students to respond to scenarios of success involving hypothetical first-year male and female medical students. The two medical students were introduced with names that clearly identified their gender, and it was reported that they had achieved top standing in their class for the first semester in medical school. The student respondents were asked to speculate about how the professional and personal lives of these two individuals would unfold as a result of their successful completion of medical school.

Males and females alike saw the male medical student as on his way to a very successful medical career, a wonderful home life with an adoring family, and many honors and personal rewards. The female medical student, on the other hand, was perceived by both male and female subjects as having no place in a male career pattern, was urged to switch to something more feminine like nursing, was accused of probably cheating her way to the top by copying the work of a male student, and destined to live an unhappy, neurotic life.

Based on the responses of the male and female subjects in her study, Horner concluded that women fear success in competitive situations and men do not.

Research in sports initially supported Horner's work, but as time has passed, it seems abundantly clear that females in sport no longer fear success: rather, they thrive on it. One can only assume that the same is true for women in all competitive situations. Horner's work has been consigned to a place in the history of the evolution of women, a poignant snapshot of where the women's movement was 40 years ago.

Psychological androgyny

Sandra Bem introduced the concept of androgyny to the psychological literature in 1974. To Bem, there were traditional female roles and expectations, traditional male ones, and those that cut across both genders, namely androgynous ones. To test this hypothesis, she created the **Bem Sex Role Inventory** (BSRI), a 60-item scale measuring masculinity, femininity, and androgyny.

TRY IT NOW!

Are you masculine, feminine, or androgynous?

Though there are several scales that are designed to assess psychological androgyny, the one that has achieved the most recognition is that of Bem, the creator of the BSRI. If you're interested in where you stand on her psychological construct, there's a website that will tell you: http://masculineheart.blogspot.com/2010/12/take-bem-sex-role-inventory.html1

As you can see from taking the BSRI, masculinity and femininity are defined in terms of traditional roles and expectations. Words and phrases such as 'tactful', 'quiet', 'aware of feelings of others', 'need for security', and 'easily expresses tender feelings' are traditional female descriptors, and are referred to as **expressive** traits. On the other hand, 'aggressive', 'independent', 'dominant', 'competitive', 'active', 'ambitious', and 'decisive' have long been used to describe males, and these are **instrumental** traits. The extent to which one endorses these descriptors determines masculinity, femininity, or androgyny. People who endorse across both these traditional lines would thus be androgynous.

In almost every study in sport, female athletes are either masculine or androgynous in their sex role endorsement. It's important to remember here that we're not talking of sexual partner preference, but rather the extent to which one endorses traditional sex role expectations.

One interesting side note to the androgyny research in sports and fitness is that women who endorse traditional femininity are at high risk for dropping out of fitness activities due to their perceptions of the strenuousness of physical activity and its more male properties. Knowing that a new client endorses a feminine sex role identity might be useful information to the fitness trainer who could then tailor exercises and expectations to fit the client.

Female attributions in sport

In its simplest form, as we saw in Chapter 7, traditional attribution theory suggests that people use four basic explanations to account for events taking place around them: **ability**, **task difficulty**, **effort**, and **luck**.

An ability attribution in sport might go along the lines of: 'I'm successful in sports. I must be a good athlete.' As for task difficulty, it's one thing to run the sprints in athletics and quite another to master the hurdles, and the attributions that arise from each situation would probably be quite different. Regarding effort, athletes and coaches often talk of success as being attributable to the fact that they outworked their opponents. Luck attributions include bad weather, the bounce of the ball, and unpredictable officiating.

 In general, male athletes have been shown to use **internal** attributions such as ability and effort to explain success, and females have often invoked **external** ones relating to task difficulty and luck. At the same time, women tend to also downplay ability in explaining success.

REMEMBER THIS!!! Female immersion in sport is a relatively recent phenomenon, and issues related to homophobia, eating disorders, and distorted or minimal media coverage remain problematic.

Research in sport psychology has focused on fear of success, psychological androgyny, and attribution theory.

15. Exercise and fitness

Facts and statistics

Estimates are that three out of every five people in the US are overweight or obese, and the picture gets worse every year. Only three per ten people receive the recommended amount of daily physical activity. Type 2 or adult diabetes is becoming more common, very much related to excess weight: 41 million Americans are pre-diabetic. Heart disease is the leading cause of death among American men and women. The typical child watches four or more hours of television each day, not to mention time spent on video games and other electronic diversions. Physical education participation in the public schools is at an all-time low.

And there appears to be evidence that this obesity picture is being repeated in other industrialized countries as the Americans export their fatty foods and sugar-laced soft drinks. For example, global estimates indicate that one seventh of the world population is overweight or obese. In Australia, estimates are that if trends continue, 80% of all adults in that country will be overweight or obese by 2020. In New Zealand, one out of every four adults are obese – and the figure is 42% for the indigenous Maori. A recent study of European Union countries found the highest obesity rates among the Germans, followed closely by the British.

These global health challenges haven't gone unnoticed by sport and exercise psychologists, who think they have something important to say about improving exercise adherence and generally promoting good health practices in all age groups.

Are the Japanese the exception to the rule?
Recent reports from the internet suggest that fitness programs are alive and well in Japan, with noted increases in the numbers of people who say they work out regularly, numbers of consistent joggers, incredible increases in application for and participation in the Tokyo Marathon, big leaps in sales of jogging shoes and exercise equipment, and substantial hikes in the sale of bicycles. It's also important to note that radio broadcasts of morning calisthenics have been a part of the work and school life of Japanese citizens since the early 1950s.

A brief history

In 1952, Dwight D. Eisenhower was elected to the American presidency. One of his many concerns was the issue of youth fitness. Eisenhower thought the country was at a crisis point regarding youth fitness, so he convened a group to assess fitness levels of Americans and compare the results with a sample of European youth. The comparisons were quite unfavorable for the American youth, and this led Eisenhower to create the President's Council on Youth Fitness, now known as the President's Council on Physical Fitness and Sports (PCPFS). Luminaries such as bodybuilder, actor, and politician Arnold Schwarzenegger, track great Florence Griffith Joyner, Hall of Fame collegiate football coach Charles 'Bud' Wilkinson, major league baseball icon Stanley Musial, and basketball coaching legend Al McGuire are among the many who have served as chairpersons of PCPFS.

Eisenhower's efforts led the American Alliance for Health, Physical Education, Recreation and Dance (AAHPERD) to create a set of tests that the organization believes is the best way to assess overall fitness. Their assessment is composed of:

- A flexed arm hang
- One-minute of bent-knee sit-ups
- A shuttle run
- A standing long jump
- A 50-yard dash
- A 600-yard run.

How would you do?

Physical activity, exercise, and physical fitness defined

Though they are often used interchangeably, fitness experts and sport psychologists differentiate among the terms physical activity, physical fitness, and exercise.

- **Physical activity** refers to any bodily movement produced by skeletal muscles that results in an expenditure of energy. A mailman outrunning the family dog, a woman weeding her flower garden, and a housewife trying to control the energy level of three pre-kindergartners are all engaging in physical activity.

- As for **exercise**, it's a sub-set of physical activity in which planned, organized, and repetitive components are involved in initiating or maintaining physical fitness.

- **Physical fitness** refers to a set of health and fitness-related skills that are made up of such things as cardio-respiratory endurance, muscular strength, muscular endurance, and flexibility.

It's the task of the physical educator, coach, fitness trainer, and sport psychologist to come up with activities and methods that create and maintain physical fitness.

What is your fitness personality?
As the introduction to the following internet assessment device says, it's not always easy to identify the type of exercise that you would enjoy the most, and that is best for you based on your personality. The fitness personality quiz attempts to provide insight into what you might profit from the most, and can be found at: http://exercise.about.com/library/blfitnesspersonalityquiz.html

Exercise adherence

The biggest challenge facing fitness experts is how to foster exercise adherence. It's well-documented that people talk a great deal about fitness, many give it a cursory try, but few actually adhere to a continuous, sound fitness program.

The physical and psychological benefits of fitness are numerous and obvious. **Physically**, a reduction in the likelihood of premature death, benefits to the cardiovascular and respiratory systems, enhancing resistance to disease, improvements in one's sex life, and better sleep habits are all possible physical outcomes. **Psychologically**, stress reduction, alleviation of depression, increased opportunities for socialization, and the plain old thrill of competing against yourself and/or others are all possible benefits. Despite these well known and often-documented advantages of exercise, some estimates suggest that at least 50% of the people who start a fitness program will drop out within six months or less. Even in cardiac patients where one would think motivation would be at a peak, exercise adherence rates are discouraging.

What, then, are some predictors of this elusive adherence?

1. **Physical proximity**. It's important to choose a workout site that is easily reached geographically. Simply stated, adherence is assisted when the workout area is nearby.

2. **Spousal support**. Where applicable, there does appear to be a mildly positive relationship between having a spouse who is supportive and continuation in an exercise program.

3. **Social support**. We are herd animals in a sense, and having the support of peers in a workout group can be of help in adherence.

4. **Small versus large workout groups**. Somewhat related to the social support theme is size of the workout group. Evidence suggests that the social reinforcement gained from small groups promotes adherence.

5. **Socio-economic status**. Blue-collar workers often get their daily dose of physical exertion through hard work, thus rendering them unlikely to pursue an organized exercise program. Also, the cost of joining many of the exercise groups is prohibitive for most at the lower end of the socio-economic ladder.

6. **Self-fulfilling prophecy**. Here we are asking people to predict their future exercise behavior, and one's expectancy of success does indeed seem to be a predictor of adherence.

Psychological predictors

It appears that there are psychological variables that affect exercise adherence, and some of the more salient are:

1. **Locus of control**. In an earlier chapter, we talked of the psychological trait known as locus of control, or where individuals see control in their environment. There is some research evidence that an internal locus of control is positively related to health behaviors such as exercise.

2. **Introversion–extraversion**. There are several psychological studies showing higher exercise compliance rates for people who are outgoing and sociable, or extraverts.

3. **Type A personality**. Some theorists and researchers have suggested that people are either Type A or Type B personalities. Type A's are aggressive, hard-charging, hard-working, impatient, and competitive, while Type B's are easy-going, laid-back, live-and-let-live kinds of people. There's a considerable literature to suggest that Type A's are prone to psychosomatic illness, most particularly coronary problems brought about by the

traits that make them Type A. (One of my colleagues has made a tongue-in-cheek suggestion that the reason Type A's have so many problems with high blood pressure and heart attacks is because Type B's are always underfoot, in the way and messing up everything.) With regard to the Type A/exercise relationship, impatience with results, the lack of immediate feedback as to the efficacy of the fitness program, the failure to endorse group exercise goals, and their general hurry-up attitude get in the way of exercise adherence for these people. Thus, Type A personalities are at high risk for dropping out of sorely needed constructive outlets for some of their excess energy.

Are you a Type A personality?
There are a number of online assessments designed to let you know if you're a Type A or Type B personality. Two such internet sources are as follows:

http://www.blogthings.com/
doyouhavetypeapersonalityquiz/

http://www.psyc.uncc.edu/pagoolka/TypeAB.html

Both instruments are simple and brief and provide a glimpse at least into the kinds of actions and behaviors that compose the Type A personality.

Strategies for improving exercise adherence

Fitness experts including sport and exercise psychologists have borrowed from the broader field of behavioral psychology in developing methods of promoting exercise adherence. One of these methods is the **behavioral contract**.

 If you're having trouble getting fit and sticking to your exercise plan, try drawing up a behavioral contract. This is where you, the exerciser, enter into a written agreement with the exercise provider to adhere to various aspects of the exercise regimen. It's one thing to verbally agree to adhere, but quite another to put it in writing and put your signature on the document. We're all a bit more prone to follow up on something if we've signed off on it as opposed to merely agreeing to do it.

Another behavioral technique is to enter into an **exercise lottery**. In the lottery, exercise is determined on a daily basis through a lottery system – the 'luck of the draw'. A variety of possible exercise programs fitted to the interests and capabilities of the exerciser may be placed in a hat and each day's exercise program will be determined via a personalized lottery.

Self-monitoring is another behavioral approach in which careful monitoring of weight loss, heart rate, blood pressure, repetitions or amounts of weights, and distance run might be included, depending on the individual and the situation.

 The self-monitoring technique makes me think of a local runner who always showed up for his daily jog wearing a T-shirt with the number of miles he had run in the past ten or fifteen years emblazoned in large letters on the back of the shirt. From time to time, he would update his shirts with the latest tally of miles accumulated.

Stimulus cueing is a fourth technique, and it emphasizes a highly organized, almost ritualistic, approach to all aspects of the exercise setting. Working out at the same time and same place each day, wearing favorite workout gear, and enjoying exercise with selected friends are all parts of stimulus cueing. The whole idea here is to systematize the workouts so that they become routine, expected parts of one's day and one's life.

 As an example of stimulus cueing, I have joined my colleagues Jack Nation and Tony Bourgeois from our Department of Psychology, in jogging five times a week over pretty much the same path for the past 35 years, always making sure that we run no more than 3 miles at no faster than an 8-minute pace. We always run at noon so as to break up the work day, make sure our classes end to fit the workout schedule, and seldom let cold, hot, or rainy weather interfere with our ritual. At some point, the jogging becomes part of your psyche and part of your soul, thus making it highly resistant to non-adherence.

Essential to all of these approaches to adherence is the concept of **reinforcement** discussed earlier. We know that by its very definition, anything that increases the likelihood of a response serves as a reinforcer, or a reward. The more rewards you can bring to the table, the more likely you are to continue to exercise. Pat yourself on the back for a job well done, keep track of the miles run, buy yourself some new wardrobe items to reward weight loss goals, systematize your workouts, and vary the pace, type, and intensity from time to time. All of these rewards stamp in fitness behaviors!

Are you an exercise addict?

Sport psychologists make a distinction between positive and negative addiction to exercise.

Positive addiction is characterized by control, competence, and a sense of well-being; exercise is thus part of one's life, blended in with work and family life. The positively addicted person controls the exercise, not the reverse.

Negative addiction, on the other hand, implies that exercise has become the master in the relationship, with the individual oblivious to the consequences of their behavior:

- they run until they drop;
- they exercise to the detriment of career, family life, and other interpersonal relationships;
- there is a need to steadily increase the amount of exercise;
- withdrawal symptoms similar to those typically associated with drug dependence are experienced;
- life events are increasingly structured to include exercise (i.e. vacations);
- injuries are minimized or ignored to the detriment of overall health.

How many of the negative symptoms do you have?

Effects of exercise on thinking and mood

Two areas of interest to sport researchers related to exercise have to do with its effects on how we **think** and how we **feel**.

With regard to the former, the research has generally supported the notion that regular exercise clears the mind of clutter and does help us think more clearly.

Even more robust are the findings related to the effects of exercise on anxiety and depression. There's no doubt that exercise has **anxiolytic** or anxiety-reducing properties, and its effect on depression is considerable. Estimates are that one person in six world-wide will suffer from some degree of depression in their lifetime, so it behooves us all to look for remedies for the condition. One such remedy appears to be found in exercise. Particularly powerful in this regard is distance running. A number of studies have been conducted on the running/depression relationship and virtually all point to the mood-elevating effects of such exercise. Running is also cost effective when compared with more standard and accepted treatments such as psychotherapy and prescription anti-depressant medications.

How does exercise reduce anxiety?

There are no panaceas or cure-alls for every case of anxiety or depression, but it does appear that exercise exerts a positive effect on overall mood. How, then, do we account for these mood escalations? Exercise physiologists and sport psychologists generally espouse four possible reasons for the anxiety-reducing effects of exercise:

1. **The distraction hypothesis**. In this formulation, it's assumed that exercise exerts its anxiety-reducing effects by distracting the person from stressors in their lives.

2. **The endorphin hypothesis**. Here, the emphasis is on the possible release of morphine-like chemicals from the brain, thus reducing physical and psychological pain

and inducing a state of euphoria or well-being. Though unproven, the theory is intriguing and continues to draw attention from top physiology researchers.

3. **The thermogenic hypothesis**. In this instance, anxiety is thought to be reduced through the elevation of body temperature. It may well be that the anxiety-reducing effects of a warm bath or a sauna also arise from this same source.

4. **The monoamine hypothesis**. This model is largely based on animal research and suggests that the anxiety-reducing effects of exercise arise from the alteration in the brain of chemical substances such as serotonin or norepinephrine.

Which of the theories, if any, do you think applies to you and exercise? (I'm particularly fond of the thermogenic hypothesis myself. I find the warming effects on the body associated with exercise to be particularly reinforcing.) None of the theories carries any more weight than another at this point, but it's likely that all will stimulate additional research to see if exercise is indeed tied in some way to any or all of them.

Exercise for senior citizens

The legendary American baseball pitcher and amateur philosopher Satchel Paige once commented: 'How old would you be if you didn't know how old you wuz?' What our distinguished philosopher was commenting on was a take-off on the idea that you're only as old as you feel. As the world population ages, more and more emphasis is being placed on sports and fitness activities for seniors. It's expected that 70 million Americans will be over the age of 65 by the year 2030. Given the even greater life expectancy of people in some of the industrialized countries of Europe and Asia, it's clear that there will be lots of senior citizens, and many will be seeking outlets through organized sports and fitness activities. This 'graying' is one of the many challenges facing the governments of these countries over the next 20 to 50 years and beyond.

One area in which gerontologists, gero-psychologists, sports and exercise psychologists, and other experts on aging can make a big contribution in the future is in devising fitness programs for seniors. There's a rich and abundant literature showing the benefits of exercise for seniors, even for those who have been sedentary for many years. With the right kinds of programs and incentives, people can literally throw away their crutches, walkers, and wheelchairs in favor of independent locomotion. Scores of studies have supported this relationship.

Health-related issues associated with a sedentary lifestyle and obesity are of near-epidemic proportions in the United States, and other countries in Europe are increasingly concerned about the fitness of their citizens. The fitness boom may be more apparent than real, and sport and exercise psychologists are working on improving exercise adherence. Regular exercise does seem to exert a positive effect on thinking, mood, anxiety, and depression. And increasingly, attention is being directed to the fitness needs of older citizens.

Appendix A

A brief history of sport psychology

Sport psychology has arguably been a field of inquiry for only a little over a hundred years. There were a couple of notable experiments conducted in psychology laboratories in the late 1800s and early 1900s with a sport theme. However, the field got a real shot in the arm in 1923 with the establishment of the first sport psychology laboratory at the University of Illinois. A young Illinois psychology professor by the name of Dr Coleman Griffith, known widely as the 'Father of Sport Psychology', developed an interest in sport psychology as a result of getting to know collegiate athletes in his introductory psychology classes. These interactions led Griffith to set up his laboratory, conduct scientific investigations into the psyche of the athlete, and write a couple of books in 1926 and 1928 with athlete and coaching themes. Later, Griffith got out of the sport psychology business and it was over 40 years before much happened of consequence.

In Dallas, Texas, in 1967, a group of physical educators with an interest in the psychological aspects of sports met and created the first professional organization devoted to sport psychology, the North American Society for the Psychology of Sport and Physical Activity (NASPSPA). Twenty years later, a more significant organization was formed, the Association for the Advancement of Applied

Sport and Physical Activity (AAASP). AAASP is now known as the Association for Applied Sport Psychology (AASP) and is the major professional organization in place today with the goal of promoting sport and exercise psychology. AASP has approximately 1,000 members and is responsible for providing training guidelines for university programs in sport psychology. As well, AASP has instituted a set of ethical principles that guide the professional behavior of professors, researchers, and practitioners. Another major contribution of AASP is its credentialing program. Members of the organization who meet stringent training standards are eligible to apply for credentialing as a Certified Consultant, Association of Applied Sport Psychology (CC-AASP). This was a response to state psychology licensing laws that were instituted in all states in the US and provinces in Canada during the 1960s, which greatly restricted who could call oneself a psychologist. AASP credentialing was designed to confer credibility on talented professionals in the field while protecting the consumer by providing them with a list of certified (but not licensed) individuals who have been held to rigorous training standards.

Coinciding with the creation of AASP in 1986 was the formation of Division 47, Sport and Exercise Psychology, within the American Psychological Association (APA). AASP and Division 47 have considerable overlap in membership and exert reasonably equal influence on teaching, research, and practice within the field in the United States. Australia, Britain, and Canada, among others, have similar advocacy groups. For example, the Australian Psychological Society has a College of Sport and Exercise Psychologists. Areas of specialization include performance enhancement and mental skills development, anxiety and stress management, overtraining and burnout, and health and wellness coaching. Similarly, the British Psychological Society sponsors divisions, sections, and special groups for its membership. A Division of Sport and Exercise Psychology was created in 2004, and one section is devoted to professionals with an interest in Coaching Psychology. And the Canadian Psychological Association has 31 sections, one of which is for Sport and Exercise. Their mission is to provide a forum for communication and information for a wide variety of professionals with an interest in sport and exercise.

Appendix B

Prominent figures in sport and exercise psychology

Any list of prominent people within a designated area is going to be arbitrary and, as a result, many important contributors will get overlooked. I have no doubt that the case is the same here. I am going to approach the list from the standpoint of important contributors in the areas of research, practice, and the writing of significant books in sport psychology.

Examples of representative research areas and prominent researchers

Albert Carron and Associates, Canada, Team and Group Cohesion; **Stuart Biddle**, Britain, Attribution Theory in Sports; **Linda Carpenter and Vivian Acosta**, Women's Sports Participation; **Packianathan Chelladurai**, The Ohio State University, Leadership in Sports; **Rod Dishman**, University of Georgia, Exercise Psychology; **Joan Duda**, Achievement Goal Theory; **Yuri Hanin**, Russia, Anxiety; **William Morgan**, University of Wisconsin, Staleness and Burnout; **Robert Nideffer**, Enhanced Performance Systems, Concentration, Focus, and Attentional Control; **Martin E.P. Seligman**, University of Pennsylvania, Learned Helplessness and Learned Optimism; **Ronald Smith** and **Frank Smoll**,

University of Washington, Youth Sport Coaching; **Robin Vealey**, Sports Self-Confidence.

Important practitioners
David Cook, Consultant to Men's Professional Golf Association (PGA) and Ladies Express, Bayer, Bristol-Myers Squibb, Compaq, Heinz, State Farm Insurance, Texas Instruments, others; **Kate Hays**, Canadian practitioner who specializes in what she calls 'Performance Psychology', who works with actors, dancers, singers, and stage performers as well as athletes; **Graham Jones**, prominent British researcher/practitioner who has consulted with numerous athletes and such corporate clients as Bourne Leisure, Coca-Cola, Dresdner Kleinwort, Deutsche Bank, and Minter Ellison; **Fran Pirozollo**, consultant to New York Yankees, Texas Rangers, and numerous professional golfers; **Robert Rotella**, prominent consultant to numerous professional golfers and author of several books and tapes on enhancing golf performance.

References

Chapter 1
The field of sport psychology: an overview

Green, C.D., & Benjamin, L.T. (eds), (2009). *Psychology gets in the game: Sport, mind, and Behavior, 1880–1960*. Lincoln, NE: University of Nebraska Press.

This book covers the historical roots of sport psychology with a series of readings by sports authorities and historians. It's engagingly written and is particularly thorough in its coverage of the early historical milestones from which the discipline arose.

Each of the following textbooks or reference works are widely used in sport psychology classes and by applied practitioners working with teams, athletes, and exercise groups. Some of the discussions in each text focus on theory and research but all authors do provide numerous examples of real-life applications of sport and exercise psychology.

Burke, K.L., Sachs, M.L., Fry, S.J., & Schweighardt, S.L. (2008). *Directory of graduate programs in applied sport psychology* (9th edn). Morgantown, WV: Fitness Information Technology.

Cox, R.H. (2012). *Sport psychology: Concepts and applications* (7th edn). New York: McGraw-Hill.

Karageorghis, C., & Terry, P. (2011). *Inside sport psychology.* Champaign, IL: Human Kinetics.

LeUnes, A. (2008). *Sport psychology* (4th edn). New York: Taylor & Francis/PsyPress.

Tenenbaum, G. (2007). *Handbook of sport psychology* (3rd edn). New York: Wiley.

Weinberg, R.S., & Gould, D. (2011). *Sport psychology,* (5th edn). Champaign, IL: Human Kinetics.

Williams, J.M. (2010). *Applied sport psychology: Personal growth to peak experience* (6th edn). New York: McGraw-Hill.

Chapter 2
Reinforcement and punishment

Martin, G., & Lumsden, J.A. (1987). *Coaching: An effective behavioral approach.* St Louis, MO: Times Mirror/ Mosby.
This old standby on coaching incorporates behavioral principles at their best. Assessment of behavior baselines, proper dispensation of reward and punishment, setting sensible and achievable goals, and strategies for dealing with problem behaviors within a team are discussed clearly and well.

Martin, G.L., & Pear, J. (2007). *Behavior modification: What it is and how to do it* (8th edn). Upper Saddle River, NJ: Prentice-Hall.
The basics of learning, positive and negative reinforcement, punishment, and other topics are treated thoroughly by the

authors, and their sport examples make this book especially useful.

Smith, R.E. (2010). 'A positive approach to coaching effectiveness and performance enhancement.' In J.M. Williams (ed.), *Applied sport psychology: Personal growth to peak experience* (6th edn), pp. 42–58. New York: McGraw-Hill.

Smith talks of the ABC's of behavior control, or the basic assumptions and principles behind the use of reward and punishment in the context of coaching. This reading is an excellent one for the beginner who would like to understand how behavioral principles apply to sports.

Chapter 3
Anxiety, arousal, and their assessment

Cox, R.H., Martens, R.P., & Russell, M.D. (2003). 'Measuring anxiety in athletics: The Revised Competitive State Anxiety Inventory-2.' *Journal of Sport & Exercise Psychology*, 25, 519–533.

This journal article reports research by these authorities on the development of their sport anxiety scale. The CSAI-2 is a popular measure of state anxiety in sports, or the kind of anxiety experienced by most of us when we are confronted with life events to which to we attach great importance. When the important event passes, state anxiety typically dissipates also.

Martens, R.P. (1977). *Sport Competition Anxiety Test*.
    Champaign, IL: Human Kinetics.
In this test manual, Martens explains the development of the
SCAT, a measure of trait anxiety in sport. In contrast to state
anxiety, trait anxiety is an enduring part of the personality
make-up of the individual; it's how the person reacts to life
events on a more permanent and less changeable basis.

Spielberger, C.D., Gorsuch, R.L., & Lushene, R.F. (1983).
    Manual for the State–Trait Anxiety Inventory. Palo
    Alto, CA: Consulting Psychologists Press.
The lead author here is a world-renowned expert on anxiety
and is given credit for starting the state–trait distinction. This
manual outlines all the research work that went into preparing
the STAI, which has been so successful in measuring anxiety
within and external to sport that it has been translated into a
number of foreign languages.

Chapter 4
Treatment of sport anxiety

Simons, J. (2000). 'Doing imagery in the field.' In
    M.B. Andersen (ed.), *Doing sport psychology*,
    pp. 79–92. Champaign, IL: Human Kinetics.
The author shows how visual imagery scripts can be used
to enhance performance by using a male collegiate discus
thrower, an elite female high jumper, and a world-ranked
javelin thrower.

Smith, R.E. (1984). 'Theoretical and treatment approaches in anxiety reduction.' In J.M. Silva & R.S. Weinberg (eds), *Psychological foundations of sport*, pp. 157–70. Champaign, IL: Human Kinetics.

This reading is still one of the finest elaborations on anxiety management in sport. Smith writes about four models for reducing anxiety: extinction, counter-conditioning, cognitive–mediational, and coping skills, and gives numerous examples on how each applies to sport performance. This is a must read for someone unfamiliar with anxiety reduction in sports.

Zaichkowsky, L.D., & Takenaka, K. (1993). 'Optimizing arousal level.' In R.N. Singer, M. Murphey, & L.K. Tennant (eds), *Handbook of research on sport psychology*, pp. 511–27. New York: Macmillan.

One of the outstanding features of this reading is its inclusion of ten 'psych-up' principles that can be used by coaches or athletes to facilitate pre-game motivation. By psyching-up, the athlete attempts to gain the competitive edge through chants, slogans, deep breathing exercises, music, energizing imagery, pep talks, and so on.

Chapter 5

Optimism in sports and exercise

Csikszentmihalyi, M. (1990). *Flow: The psychology of optimal experience*. New York: Harper & Row.

Though he doesn't write specifically on positive psychology by title, Csikszentmihalyi (pronounced Chick-Sent-Me-Hi-Ya) is widely regarded as an authority on the topic. Much of his writing focuses on *flow* or a state of great absorption, engagement, and oneness with the immediate surroundings. There is similarity between being in a flow state and being 'in the zone', as athletes are prone to call it.

Seligman, M.E.P. (1991). *Learned optimism*. New York: Knopf.
Seligman is the leading expert in learned optimism and positive psychology. He is an excellent scientist and theorist, and this book serves as a departure from his earlier work on learned helplessness, a leading theory of the genesis of depression. Included in the book is an assessment device known as the Learned Optimism Test (LOT) which Seligman has developed. A variant of the LOT can be found at: http://www.stanford.edu/class/msande271/onlinetools/LearnedOpt.html

Seligman, M.E.P., Nolen-Hoeksema, S., Thornton, N., & Thornton, K.M. (1990). 'Explanatory style as a mechanism of disappointing athletic experience.' *Psychological Science*, 1, 534–41.
It's Seligman's contention that optimistic athletes fare far better in sports than do athletes with a more pessimistic style, and he supports this contention with several related studies.

Chapter 6

Mental toughness in sports

Mental toughness is one of the most talked-about topics in sport psychology and it's accompanied by plenty of professional literature. There are numerous articles and books on mental toughness that have been written with the layman in mind. For example:

Crust, L., Nesti, M., & Littlewood, M. (2010). 'Player and coach ratings of mental toughness in an elite association football academy.' *Athletic Insight*: http://www.athleticinsight.com/Vol121ss3/Football.html

Jones, J.G. (2007). *Mental toughness: The mindset behind sporting achievement*. Oxford, UK: How To Books Ltd.

Jones, J.G. (2010). *Developing mental toughness: Gold medal strategies for transforming your business performance*. Miami, FL: Spring Hill Books.

Kuehl, K., Kuehl, J., & Tefertiller, C. (2006). *Mental toughness: Baseball's winning edge*. Lanham, MD: Ivan R. Dee.

Lefkowits, J., McDuff, D.R., & Riismandel, C. (no date). 'Mental toughness training manual for soccer.' http://www.cincinnatiunitedsoccer.com/Portals

Selk, J. (2008). *10-minute toughness: The mental training program for winning before the game begins*. New York: McGraw-Hill.

Sheard, M. (2010). *The mindset behind sporting achievement*. New York: Routledge.

Chapter 7

Attribution theory and locus of control

Biddle, S.J.H., Hanrahan, S.J., & Sellars, C.N. (2001).
'Attributions: Past, present, and future.' In R.N. Singer,
H.A. Hausenblas, & C.M. Janelle (eds), *Handbook of
sport psychology* (2nd edn), pp. 444–71. New York:
Wiley.

This paper provides a nice summary of the status of attribution
theory up to 2001. The material on assessment issues and
attributional retraining is particularly interesting and relevant to
sport psychology.

Levenson, H. (1981). 'Differentiating among internality,
powerful others, and chance.' In H. Lefcourt (ed.),
*Research with the locus of control construct:
Assessment Methods* (Vol. 1), pp. 1–39. New York:
Academic Press.

Levenson's scale is one of the two major locus of control
assessment devices in use today. Her broadening of the locus
of control construct to include powerful others and chance as
sub-dimensions of an external locus was groundbreaking at the
time it first was published.

Rotter, J. (1971). 'External control and internal control.'
Psychology Today, 5(1), 37–42, 58–9.

Rotter was the first to introduce locus of control theory to the
psychological literature and his I-E Scale, along with Levenson's
scale, are the two most popular assessment devices available.

Chapter 8

Leadership, group cohesion, and audience effects

Carron, A.V., Hausenblas, H., & Eys, M. (2005). *Group dynamics in sport* (3rd edn). Morgantown, WV: Fitness Information Technology.

Carron is widely regarded as the foremost authority in sport psychology on group dynamics. He and his colleagues have created the definitive work on group dynamics with discussions of such topics as leadership, team building, goal setting, and group cohesion. This is a must read for someone interested in the group dynamics of sports teams.

Chelladurai, P. (1989). *Manual for the Leadership Scale for Sports*. Columbus, OH: The Ohio State University.

Chelladurai has long reigned as the leading theorist and researcher in sports leadership, and this manual discusses at length the Leadership Scale for Sports (LSS), which has been used in dozens of published studies over the past several decades.

Cialdini, R.B., Borden, R.J., Thorne, A., Walker, M.R., Freeman, S., and Sloan, L.R. (1976). 'Basking in reflected glory: Three (football) field studies.' *Journal of Personality and Social Psychology*, 34, 366–75.

In a classic research piece, the authors devised an ingenious design showing that fans really do identify with winners (what they called 'BIRGing', or Basking in Reflected Glory) and try to distance themselves from losers ('CORFing', or Cutting off Reflected Failure).

Chapter 9
Team building and goal setting

Dale, G., & Conant, S. (2004). *101 teambuilding activities: Ideas every coach can use to enhance teamwork, communication and trust.* Cary, NC: Janssen Peak Performance, Inc.

The title gives this book away: a book full of proven activities that coaches can use to build team unity. They are fun, applicable, and have been used over and over with athletic teams and corporate teams.

Janssen, J. (2002). *Championship team building: What every coach needs to know to build a motivated, committed and cohesive team.* Cary, NC: Janssen Peak Performance, Inc.

Janssen is a leading authority on sports leadership and team building. He conducts workshops all over the country on leadership and team building, and his book is a summary of his philosophy about those two topics.

Sivils, K., & Jones, P. (2011). *Goal setting for sport: A concise guide for coaches and athletes.* Seattle, WA: Create Space.

Sivils has many years of coaching experience and this book is his attempt to synthesize and refine his theory of the role of goal setting as a means of promoting team harmony, team success, and player enjoyment. He discusses ten steps he thinks are essential aspects of goal setting, and pitfalls to be avoided.

Chapter 10
Aggression and violence in sports

Bandura, A. (1973). *Aggression: A social learning analysis.* Englewood Cliffs, NJ: Prentice-Hall.

There are two major positions in psychology concerning the expression of aggression, one of which asserts that expressing aggression lowers aggressive acts. Bandura is the major spokesman for the other position, which states that expressing aggression reinforces aggressive acts, thus making them more likely, not less so.

Benedict, J., & Yaeger, D. (1998). *Pros and cons: The criminals who play in the NFL.* New York: Warner Books.

The authors looked at the criminal records of 109 professional football players for the 1996–97 season and found that two were arrested for murder, seven for rape, 42 for assault and battery, and 45 for domestic violence. The NFL has chastised the authors for unnecessarily stigmatizing players in the league.

Rainey, D. (1986). 'A gender difference in acceptance of sport aggression: A classroom activity.' *Teaching of Psychology*, 13, 138–140.

A particularly appealing feature of this brief article is Rainey's inclusion of six aggression scenarios, which I find very useful in introducing the topic of aggression in my sport psychology classes. Rainey did find that females scored lower with regard to their endorsement or acceptance of the six scenarios.

Chapter 11
Psychological assessment

LeUnes, A. (2002). *Journal citations of psychological tests used in sport and exercise psychology research.* Lewiston, NY: Mellen Press.

This collection is made up of 2,300 citations listed by test, author, and sport, and is designed to facilitate research in sport and exercise psychology by reducing the legwork an investigator might have to engage in to conduct his or her work.

Lorr, M., McNair, D.M., Heuchert, J.W.P., & Droppleman, L.F. (2003). *Profile of Mood States Manual.* North Tonawanda, NY: Multi-Health Systems, Inc.

This scale has been around since 1971 and has been used to assess mood in psychiatric clients, a huge variety of medical patients, normal adults, college students, and sports and exercise participants. Of particular interest here is the latter group, which has been the focus of well over 500 published research studies.

Ostrow, A.C. (ed.), (2002). *Directory of psychological tests in the sport and exercise sciences* (2nd edn). Morgantown, WV: Fitness Information Technology.

There are 314 psychological tests, scales, and questionnaires listed here, and they are divided into major research domains such as aggression, anxiety, attribution theory, body image, cohesion, sport self-confidence, leadership, and locus of control.

Chapter 12
Risk-sport athletes, injured athletes, black athletes

Entine, J. (2000). *Why black athletes dominate sport and why we are afraid to talk about it*. New York: Public Affairs.

Entine writes about why black athletes are so dominant in some, though not all, sports. He makes a strong case that many of the differences that have long been thought to be psychosocial are actually biological. There has been much debate about his assertions.

Krakauer, J. (1997). *Into Thin Air*. Santa Monica, CA: Villard.

Jon Krakauer recounts his experiences when he joined a team of climbers set on conquering Mount Everest, the most challenging climb in the world. A storm left six climbers dead and two others were abandoned.

Pargman, D. (ed.), (2007). *Psychological bases of sports injuries* (3rd edn). Morgantown, WV: Fitness Information Technology.
Topics discussed include injury assessment, treatment ethics, malingering athletes, psychological treatment strategies, and suicide among athletes.

Chapter 13
Youth sport

DuBois, R. (1980). 'Competition in youth sport: Process or product?' *Physical Educator*, 37, 151–54.
The author has laid out a framework for understanding motives in youth sport. A product orientation is built around winning at all costs, winning awards, and dehumanizing the opponents. A process orientation focuses on good sportsmanship, playing for the fun of it, and valuing the opponents without whom there would be no contest.

Hyman, M. (2009). *Until it hurts: America's obsession with youth sports and how it harms our kids*. Boston, MA: Beacon Press.
Hyman is a journalist, coach, and sports dad who has written an eye-opening book about how parents are corrupting the youth sport experience with their over-emphasis on winning, non-stop year-round participation, misbehavior at events, and endless professionalization.

Putney, C. (2001). *Muscular Christianity: Manhood and sports in Protestant America*. Cambridge, MA: Harvard University Press.

The author traces the Muscular Christianity movement, which dominated the thinking of physical educators and the clergy during the late 1800s and early 1900s. The movement focused on the powers of sports and exercise in channeling youthful urges and energies in constructive, faith-based ways.

Chapter 14
Women in sport

Carpenter, L.J., & Acosta, R.V. (2005). *Title IX*. Champaign, IL: Human Kinetics.

The authors have chronicled the history of women's sports since the passage of the Title IX legislation in 1971 that revolutionized sports participation opportunities for women in the US.

Cayleff, S.E. (1995). *Babe: The life and legend of Babe Didrikson Zaharias*. Urbana, IL: University of Illinois Press.

This is an engaging biography of the best woman athlete ever. Her successes in track and field, softball, basketball, and golf are chronicled in the context of repressive attitudes about women participating in sport in the 1930s and 40s.

Ryan, J. (1995). *Little girls in pretty boxes: The making and breaking of elite gymnasts and figure skaters*. New York: Doubleday.

This is a grim account of the exploitation of young gymnasts and figure skaters by their parents, coaches, and sports administrators. Numerous accounts of dreams gone awry in the face of serious injuries and severe eating disorders abound in this inside look at these two sports.

Chapter 15
Exercise and fitness

Berger, B., Pargman, D., & Weinberg, R. (2006). *Foundations of exercise psychology*. Morgantown, WV: Fitness Information Technology.

This text provides an excellent foundation for understanding the nuances of exercise psychology. Interesting coverage of gender issues, exercise for children, exercising seniors, and the dangers associated with excessive exercising.

Lox, C.L., Martin Ginis, K.A., & Petruzzello, S.J. (2006). *The psychology of exercise: Integrating theory and practice*. Scottsdale, AZ: Holcomb Hathaway.

The second half of the book is particularly interesting with its coverage of body image, anxiety, depression, emotional well-being, self-concept, and quality of life issues.

McNab, T. (1982). *Flanagan's Run*. New York: William Morrow & Company.

The author has written a humorous, sensitive novel based on an ultramarathon race in 1928 in which the participants ran from Los Angeles, California, to New York City. McNab has populated the book with a fascinating collection of fictional but believable characters.

Index